THE BABY BOOMERS
GUIDE TO
TRUSTS

YOUR ALL-PURPOSE
ESTATE PLANNING TOOL

HARRY S. MARGOLIS

THE BABY BOOMERS GUIDE TO TRUSTS
YOUR ALL-PURPOSE ESTATE PLANNING TOOL
HARRY S. MARGOLIS

Ducks in a Row Publishing
Published by Ducks in a Row Publishing
Wellesley, Massachusetts

Copyediting: Julie Hills
Cover and Interior design: Yvonne Parks, PearCreative.ca
Proofreading: Lynette Smith, AllMyBest.com
Index: Jeff Evans

Library of Congress Control Number: 2021910727

Paperback ISBN: 978-1-7339310-6-9
Kindle ISBN: 978-1-7339310-7-6
ePub ISBN: 978-1-7339310-8-3

DEDICATION

To my mother, who led the way in writing books.

CONTENTS

PREFACE

War, huh
Yeah!
What is it good for?
Absolutely nothing.

EDWIN STARR

In writing this book, I kept thinking of a variation on the anti–Vietnam War anthem familiar to most members of my generation (and many others who have come since). In contrast to war, which to Edwin Starr and many others, is "good for absolutely nothing," trusts are good for just about anything in the field of estate planning—and not just for the very wealthy. Trusts are so useful that I think of them as the Swiss army knife of estate planning: they serve as a wide variety of excellent tools to accomplish any equally wide variety of goals.

Trusts can help with:

- Probate avoidance

- Asset management

- Investment oversight

- Planning for minor children

- Planning for children with disabilities

- Qualifying for public benefits

- Asset protection

- Estate tax minimization

- Planning for incapacity

- Protecting assets from Medicaid spend down or estate recovery

- Shared ownership of real estate

- Management of vacation property for families

- Shared ownership of family businesses

- Providing for pets after death

Given the myriad goals trusts can serve, they also vary considerably. As a result, many beneficiaries and trustees misunderstand and mis-administer the trusts they create, manage or benefit from.

This book aims to demystify the nuances of trusts, clearing up these misunderstandings as much as possible for all parties, grantors, trustees and beneficiaries. It was prompted by questions to my AskHarry.info website, 80 percent of which seem to be about trusts—particularly about trustee compensation. (If this is your query, don't worry: Chapter 9 has you covered.)

Through detailed explanations and examples, this book will enlarge your understanding of how trusts might accomplish your estate planning goals and serve your particular circumstances. It will provide links to additional resources and supports that might be helpful along the way. And it will help you decide whether you can create a trust on your own to suit your needs, or whether your situation warrants an investment in the guidance and expertise of an estate planning attorney.

Let's dive right in and see what this tool can do for you.

SECTION 1
THE BASICS

CHAPTER 1

WHAT IS A TRUST?

While most people have heard of a trust, few can define one succinctly. That will be our first order of business.

Trusts are legal entities that allow one or more people—the trustees—to manage assets on behalf of others—the beneficiaries—as provided by written instructions in the trust document. You might think of them as new independent financial and legal individuals. They can own property, can enter into contracts, and in some instances must pay taxes. As you will learn in this book, there are dozens of types of trusts serving a wide variety of purposes.

The trust document, often referred to as the "indenture of trust" or "trust agreement," is the rulebook or recipe that the trustee must follow. It allows tremendous flexibility. The person creating the trust, often called the "grantor" or "donor," can set the rules however they want (within reason).

Even though the trust is a paper document, you can think of it as a box or container. Its terms and the trustee's control apply only to those assets or property placed in the trust. If they're not in the box, the trust rules don't apply to them. Assets get placed in the trust by retitling them. For instance, a bank or investment account no longer will be in the name of John Doe, but instead will be titled as "John Doe as trustee of The John Doe Revocable Trust." Real estate gets transferred into a trust through a new deed.

Taking this step is very important. We've seen cases in our office where clients have very well-drafted trusts, but property ends up passing to people other than those they intended because it was never titled in the name of the trust.

While I said above that the trust document sets the rules that govern the management and use of the trust property, this is only part of the story. There are also laws that apply, both common law and statutes. The common law is the body of law created by court decisions with respect to trusts dating back at least to the 12th century when landowners going off to fight in the crusades would temporarily transfer title to their property to someone else to manage it in their absence.

That's right: although the United States declared its independence from England in 1776, its British-trained lawyers and judges continued to base their arguments and decisions on British precedents. Over the years, these have been superseded by American court decisions, so it's quite rare that you'll find any lawyer or judge citing ancient British law. But the Anglo-American legal tradition of going back to old court decisions to determine how the law applies to particular situations continues to apply.

Nevertheless, the common law rules have been superseded in large part by state laws regarding trusts, with 34 states having adopted some form of the Uniform Trust Code (UTC), a model set of laws created by a national commission. In those states, the UTC governs most aspects of trust administration, including issues such as the types of notice that must be provided to beneficiaries.

CHAPTER 2
THE PLAYERS

While trusts are written documents, they create and define roles for certain players. All trusts have one or more:

- **grantors** or donors who create and fund the trusts,

- **trustees** who manage them, and

- **beneficiaries** for whom the trust is created and managed.

Some trusts also have trust protectors in name or function.

GRANTOR

The person or people who create the trust are called the "grantor," "donor" or, in some instances, the "trustor." They decide the terms of the trust and donate property to the trust, which can be real estate or other assets, such as bank and investment accounts. They also often retain certain rights over the trust: the right to change beneficiaries, the right to hire and fire trustees, and—in the case of a revocable trust—the right to change the trust entirely or revoke it and take back the trust property.

In some cases, trusts do not have a clear grantor. Trustees can simply create the trust through a declaration of trust, which in every other way is no different from other trusts. While these trusts do not have a specific grantor or donor, for tax purposes the individual transferring funds into the trust will be deemed to be the grantor. (See Chapter 10 for a discussion of this deeming on trust taxation.)

It's also possible, though less usual, for people in addition to the grantor to make contributions to the trust. For instance, parents may create a special needs trust for the benefit of a child with a disability, and grandparents might contribute to the trust as part of their estate plan. The parents would still be considered the "grantors" of the trust.

TRUSTEE

The individuals or corporations—banks or trust companies—named as trustees must manage the trust property under the terms set out in the trust document. A trust may have a single trustee or two or more co-trustees. If there are multiple trustees, in most cases decisions must be made by consensus, but the trust can provide that, when there are three or more trustees, a majority can decide any conflicts.

While trustees can divvy up specific trustee functions among themselves—for instance, the corporate trustee handling all administrative and investment decisions and the family member trustees communicating with the beneficiaries—they all continue to have responsibility for all trust actions or inactions. A trustee cannot relieve itself of responsibility and liability by delegating it to other trustees.

BENEFICIARIES

While it seems obvious that the beneficiaries are those who benefit from the trust, it's actually a bit more complicated because different beneficiaries may have separate or overlapping interests in the trust. Those interests may be separated by time; for instance, the trust may be for the benefit of Sam during his life, but pass to his children after his death. The interests of the children may be certain—"vested" in trust terminology—or Sam might have the right to change them, in which case their interest is uncertain, or not "vested." By definition, no beneficiary of a revocable trust has a vested interest during the grantor's life since the grantor can always change the trust as she sees fit.

Beneficiaries also may have different kinds of interests. For instance, a trust may say that the income will be distributed to one or more people during their lives and then the principal will pass to others after their income beneficiaries have died. In such a case, the trustee must balance the interest of the "lifetime beneficiaries" (through trust investments that produce as much income as possible) with the interest of the so-called "remainder beneficiaries" (by preserving and increasing the value of the trust property).

In other cases, a beneficiary may have the right during his life to live in real estate owned by the trust, but for the property to pass to the so-called "remainder" beneficiaries when he dies or moves out.

TRUST PROTECTOR

In recent years, a new role has emerged in some trusts in addition to the grantor, trustee, and beneficiary: that of *trust protector*. In some cases, this is simply giving a title to roles or powers that already exist in many trusts, such as the power to remove and name trustees and the power to review and approve (or object to) accounts prepared by trustees. These oversight roles are now sometimes placed in the hands of the trust protector. However, the more significant power often given to trust protectors is the power to amend the trust itself.

This role grew up in the field of offshore asset protection trusts. Generally for wealthy people at some risk of being sued—think surgeons and people in some risky types of business—these trusts are created in foreign countries, often small islands, and operate under their laws. One of the requirements often is that the grantor give up all control over the trust and the property it holds, including the right to change trustees or to change the terms of the trust in the event of changing circumstances. That is a great risk that could discourage many potential clients from taking advantage of this asset protection option. So, creative estate planners came up with the concept of the trust protector through which the grantor can appoint someone he trusts to fill this role.

More recently, the trust protector role has become more frequently adopted and used in less exotic circumstances, often for special needs trusts and domestic asset protection trusts, which many states now permit. In both cases, the grantor has to give up control but may be concerned about the future conduct of named trustees or the need to change the trust terms if circumstances change. In the case of special needs trusts, public benefit programs are known to change their rules, requiring that trusts be amended in order to maintain the beneficiaries' continuing eligibility for coverage. In addition, the trusts may appoint independent third parties as trustees but want a family member or attorney to be able to review accounts to keep an eye on the trustee and to be able to replace the trustee if necessary.

CHAPTER 3

REVOCABLE VS. IRREVOCABLE VS. TESTAMENTARY TRUSTS

Trusts come in three basic forms: revocable, irrevocable, and testamentary. At first blush, the difference between revocable and irrevocable trusts is quite straightforward: Revocable trusts can be revoked or amended and irrevocable ones can't be. But in a closer look, the differences can be more nuanced.

REVOCABLE TRUSTS

Revocable trusts allow the grantor to change (amend) the trust agreement at any time or completely dissolve it and remove the assets it contains.

Since revocable trusts typically can be revoked or amended only by the grantors, they become irrevocable after their death when the grantors are no longer around to revoke or amend the trust. This can be confusing because the title of the trust may still read "The John Doe Revocable Trust," even though the trust is no longer revocable. (As a result, in our office we've stopped using the word "revocable" in titling revocable trusts.)

IRREVOCABLE TRUSTS

Irrevocable trusts are so named because once the trust is created, it (generally) cannot be changed or dissolved by the grantor. Why would anyone want to give up such control? Because a number of legal benefits can result, including shielding assets from taxation and permitting the grantor to qualify for public benefits. In addition, as is mentioned above, revocable trusts that continue after the death of the grantor become irrevocable.

Yet surprisingly, some irrevocable trusts are in fact amendable—just not by the grantor. For asset protection purposes, the grantor of a trust may have to give up all control. But he may be concerned that the law may change requiring an adjustment in the trust or his family situation may change in the future, meaning he may want to change trust beneficiaries. While he may not be able to make these changes himself, he may give such power to a "trust protector" (see Chapter 2). This way, changes even in an irrevocable trust can be made when and if necessary.

Another instance where an irrevocable trust may need to be changed is with special needs trusts that must satisfy the requirements of various public benefit programs, such as Medicaid and Supplemental Security Income (SSI). The federal government and state agencies may change the laws around these programs or their interpretation of existing law, requiring the trust to be modified to fit with the new law, regulation, or interpretation. The trust may provide that the trustees or trust protector can make such administrative changes so long as the changes do not affect the beneficiaries' interests. For instance, a state Medicaid agency may introduce a new requirement that trust documents include specific language that wasn't required when the trust was originally drafted.

Irrevocable trusts have always been changeable by courts through reformation actions. In general, the parties pursuing the reformation must prove that the change is necessary to carry out the original purpose of the trust. Often these actions have been brought to make sure the trust qualifies for certain tax treatment despite a change in the tax law.

More recently with widespread adoption of the Uniform Trust Code (UTC), irrevocable trusts can be modified without court approval if the grantor (if still alive) and all the beneficiaries agree. The UTC allows such modification "even if the modification or termination is inconsistent with a material purpose of the trust." An important question with respect to such modifications is which beneficiaries must consent. If a trust is for the benefit of Ann during her life and will distribute to Ann's children upon her death, or to the children of any child who predeceases Ann (her grandchildren), do the grandchildren have to approve a modification as well as their parents, since such parents may die before Ann? The answer may depend on the type of modification proposed. If it's mostly administrative in nature, the grandchildren may not need to be involved. But if, for instance, the trust is to end before Ann's death with the funds distributed outright to her children now, the grandchildren's consent may be necessary.

Another way to, in effect, modify irrevocable trusts is by "decanting" the trust assets into a new trust with new provisions. The word *decanting* comes from the fine wine practice of pouring wine from its original bottle into a new one to allow it to breathe before drinking and to leave any sediments in the original bottle. Its use in reference to trusts has grown in recent years as the practice has been permitted in many states through court decisions or specific decanting statutes. As with trust modifications pursuant to the UTC, these court rulings and statutes generally require that the new trust continue to serve the purposes for which the original trust was created and that affected parties be notified and consent to the change. One benefit of decanting over trust modification where it's allowed is that it generally does not require court action, simply notice to the beneficiaries.

In short, even presumptively irrevocable trusts may be revocable or amendable under the terms of the trust or if all the parties agree.

And even without going to the lengths of amending or decanting a trust, many grantors either retain the right to change beneficiaries or give that right to interim beneficiaries through a power of appointment. A power of appointment allows the grantor to retain the right to change beneficiaries and direct who will receive trust property upon his death, typically through a provision in his will. The trust may also give a beneficiary this right. For example, a grantor may create a trust for the benefit of her son for his life with what remains at his death to be paid to his children. It might give him the right to change who ultimately receives such trust assets. This can be very important since we can't predict what will happen several decades in the future. A grandchild may have a drug addiction and be harmed by the receipt of an inheritance. Powers of appointment are discussed in more detail in Chapter 6.

TESTAMENTARY TRUSTS

Testamentary trusts are a third kind of trust (or a second kind of irrevocable trust). These are trusts created as part of wills.

No doubt, you've heard wills titled as "Last Will and Testament," leading to the term *testamentary*. Such trusts operate no differently from other trusts, except that the probate court may retain jurisdiction, meaning that the trustee must continue to file annual accounts with the court and seek their allowance, adding to the costs of administration. The level of court oversight differs from state to state. We also find that these trusts often do not contain the same level of detail in trust terms as do most stand-alone trusts, sometimes leading to ambiguity that may have to be resolved by returning to court for instructions.

To avoid the cost and administrative burden of a testamentary trust, most estate planning attorneys recommend avoiding them, except in the case of Medicaid planning for spouses, for reasons explained in Chapter 12. Instead, they recommend using "pour-over" wills, which direct that any probate funds be distributed (poured over) to a separate trust. New York seems to be an outlier on this, with most planning involving the use of testamentary trusts.

CHAPTER 4
WHAT PURPOSES DOES A TRUST SERVE?

As we discussed at the outset, trusts are the Swiss army knives of estate planning, meaning that they can be used to serve many purposes. Often, single trusts aim to achieve several goals. While we'll explain some of these here, the second section of this book gets much more specific on the principal types of trust you are likely to encounter.

PROBATE AVOIDANCE

Wills only direct the distribution of probate property, which is property solely owned by the person who died. Other property passes automatically at death. This includes jointly owned accounts or real estate, retirement and investment accounts with a named beneficiary, life insurance (unless there's no beneficiary), and trust property. Trust property may pass to beneficiaries named in the trust, or the trust may continue for their benefit.

Avoiding probate usually makes the process simpler, quicker, and cheaper. The heirs do not have to wait for a personal representative to be approved by the probate court and then for him to gain access to the decedent's various accounts. The personal representative does not have to file accountings with the probate court or get court approval for the sale of real estate. All of this saves money and time and keeps matters private. On the other hand, it also means there's less oversight to make sure everything is on the up and up.

ASSET MANAGEMENT

Trusts help with asset management in two ways. First, the act of funding the trust—retitling assets in the name of the trust—often prompts grantors to consolidate their investment assets. It isn't unusual for clients to have their bank accounts and investments scattered among many institutions. We have found that the task of transferring title to trusts causes clients to title all their investments in a single account, which makes it a lot easier for them to see and manage what they actually own. Ultimately, when they pass away, it also makes it a lot easier for their heirs, who can deal with a single account and investment house rather than several.

The second asset management benefit of trusts is that they name co-trustees or successor trustees who can assist with managing the trust property or step in easily if or when the original trustee becomes incapacitated. Very often, two heads are better than one.

INVESTMENT OVERSIGHT

This overlaps with asset management. Consolidated management of trust assets permits better investment decisions because it makes it easier to see all of one's investments in one place. In addition, a co-trustee with investment experience or an investment manager for the trust can help make sure that the trust makes wise investment decisions. This is especially important in difficult financial situations such as the great recession and the stock market correction seen in response to the coronavirus.

When the stock market dropped precipitously upon the advent of the coronavirus pandemic, I had one beneficiary of a trust who was vehement about cashing out all of her trust's stock market investments which I resisted because doing so would lock in the losses the trust had already incurred. While I could not be certain that the market would not drop further, there's a long history that suggests that a balanced portfolio works out best in the long run, no matter the ups and downs from month to month or year to year. My young trust beneficiary did not have the experience of such history, just the panic of seeing her account total drop suddenly.

PLANNING FOR MINOR CHILDREN

It probably goes without saying that minor children cannot manage real estate, savings, or investment assets themselves. By law, parents are their natural guardians and can manage their children's assets on their behalf. Gifts to minors can be held in Uniform Transfers to Minors Accounts (UTMA) to be managed by designated third parties until the minors reach age 18 or 21, depending on the state.

If parents have passed away or become incapacitated, the probate court can appoint a guardian to make medical and living decisions and a conservator to make legal and financial decisions for minors. A conservatorship, which requires annual reporting to the probate court and other bureaucratic red tape, can be avoided if any assets to be left to minor children are instead left in trust for their benefit. This also avoids the risk that a young person will gain access to significant assets at age 18 or 21, when they may not be ready to take on this responsibility or when having the assets titled in their own name may adversely affect their eligibility for financial assistance at college.

When parents have more than one child, they often use what estate planning attorneys call a "pot" trust for their benefit. (No, it's not for buying cannabis.) Instead, the concept is that the whole family is treated as a single unit with the trustee using the funds for the benefit of the children as the trustee deems appropriate, without accounting for who receives what. Where there isn't a large age difference among the children, these trusts often end when the youngest child reaches age 25, or at least the pot trust ends and at that time the assets are divided into separate shares for each of the children. In the latter case, the trust may distribute out to the children when they reach certain ages, perhaps a third each at ages 25, 30 and 35, or continue for their benefit for asset and divorce protection purposes. (See section on asset protection in this chapter.)

PLANNING FOR CHILDREN WITH DISABILITIES

For many of the same reasons that trusts make sense for minor children, they also make sense for children of any age who have disabilities. If they have cognitive or emotional challenges, they may not be able to manage the funds or may be subject to scams or manipulation. Those with any kind of disability may depend on public benefits programs such as Supplemental Security Income, Medicaid, or Section 8 to help pay for their living expenses and medical care. Money in their own names might disqualify them or have to be used up before they can qualify for benefits. Using a special needs trust can permit them to qualify for public benefits and still have the benefit of funds left for them by their parents. See Chapter 13 for a much more expansive discussion of special needs trusts.

QUALIFYING FOR PUBLIC BENEFITS

Qualifying for public benefits is one role of special needs trusts described above. That discussion centered on trusts created by parents for their children. In certain circumstances, trusts can also be used to shelter one's own assets in order to qualify for public benefits, whether as needed due to a disability or for Medicaid coverage of long-term care costs (recognizing, of course, that the need for long-term care, whether due to cognitive decline or illness, is also due to a disability). In certain circumstances, individuals can create trusts for their own benefit or for that of a spouse and still qualify for public benefit programs. They may also want to create trusts for others who may need to qualify for public benefits now or in the future. For instance, an estate plan that leaves funds for a sibling who is in her later years perhaps should use a trust for her benefit, both for management purposes in the event her cognitive abilities decline and, if necessary, so she can qualify for Medicaid long-term care coverage without spending down the inherited funds. These trusts are discussed in more detail in Chapters 12 and 13.

ASSET PROTECTION

Trusts can be used to shelter assets from claim, whether in litigation, bankruptcy, or divorce proceedings. These trusts come in two different forms, depending on the source of the assets to be protected. So-called "third-party" trusts can shelter assets coming from someone other than the person being sued, often from a parent or grandparent. If such trusts are structured as "spendthrift" or "generation-skipping" trusts, they can offer ample protection of the assets they hold. This is discussed in more detail in Chapter 15.

It is more difficult to protect your own assets from claim if you are sued or get divorced. The common law doctrine was that, to the extent you could benefit from a trust you created or funded (or, in most cases, both), the property in trust could also benefit your creditors. A number of small island nations around the world passed laws permitting the creation of self-settled asset protection trusts, hoping to create business for their economies. This worked, and offshore trusts became a vehicle for asset protection, generally for wealthy people who could afford the high cost of setting up and maintaining them.

In more recent years, states around the country, starting with Alaska, South Dakota, and Delaware, have gotten into the act by passing laws overturning the common law and permitting the creation of domestic asset protection trusts, or DAPTs. While these are much less expensive and less cumbersome to operate than offshore trusts, they still carry some cost of creation and administration that will discourage most people from using them. Another deterrent is that the owner must give up control of her property placed in trust. Finally, you need to plan in advance; you cannot use a DAPT to protect your assets from existing claims, only from future ones. We have a more thorough discussion of both offshore and domestic asset protection trusts in Chapter 14.

ESTATE TAX MINIMIZATION

With the federal estate tax exemption currently set at $11.7 million (in 2021) for individuals and at $23.4 million for couples, it's of no concern for almost everyone. However, a number of states still have their own estate taxes with much lower limits, as low as $1 million in Massachusetts and Oregon. Trusts can be used to reduce or eliminate estate taxes in two distinct, but similar ways.

The first is a standard planning technique for married couples. Instead of holding all their assets jointly and having them pass to the other when the first passes away, they separate them into two trusts. Then after the first spouse passes away, his trust continues for the benefit of the surviving spouse, but is not included in her estate when she passes away. A simple example will demonstrate how this works. Let's assume the couple has $2 million in assets and lives in a state with a $1 million estate tax threshold. If they do no planning, the surviving spouse will end up with $2 million and the excess over $1 million will be taxed at her death. In this example, the tax could be completely avoided if they divided their assets in half so that the $1 million of the first spouse to die stays in trust for the surviving spouse, and when she dies her estate (with appropriate planning) is just under the $1 million threshold, avoiding the estate tax.

The second use of trusts in estate tax planning is less common. It involves leaving funds passing to children and grandchildren in trust for their benefit rather than giving such property to them outright. The funds in these trusts then are not taxed when the children or grandchildren pass away. While this is an added benefit of the family protection trusts described in Chapter 15, it is not the driving force behind such trusts (except for the wealthiest among us). And, for the wealthiest, it gets a bit more complicated since they may be subject to the generation-skipping tax, which is in place to prevent large estates from totally avoiding taxes when the second generation passes away.

PLANNING FOR INCAPACITY

Revocable trusts are ideal devices for planning for incapacity because the trustee can step in almost seamlessly to manage the property in trust. You may well ask, isn't that what a durable power of attorney is for? And the answer is "yes," but trusts often work better for the following reasons:

Banks and investment houses prefer them. They often put up roadblocks to the use of durable powers of attorney.

You can name successor trustees and co-trustees. If you name a co-trustee, they can sign on to all the trust accounts ahead of time, while you still manage the trust as long as you're able to do so. Then they can step in and begin to help out as needed.

Having a co-trustee waiting in the wings can also provide protection from the scams increasingly targeting seniors. The co-trustee can monitor your accounts and see when unusual sums are being withdrawn, stepping in if necessary. (Of course, this means a certain lack of privacy on your part.)

If you don't have an individual you trust to serve as your agent under a durable power of attorney, you can name a professional successor trustee or co-trustee.

Even if you do have an individual who would look out for your best interests, they may not be great at handling investments. Again, a professional successor trustee or co-trustee would be able to take care of your finances, reducing the burden on the person acting as your agent under your durable power of attorney.

PROTECTING ASSETS FROM MEDICAID SPEND DOWN OR ESTATE RECOVERY

In the realm of long-term care planning, seniors and people with disabilities use trusts in three ways. First, they can shelter their home and other assets from having to be spent down or from Medicaid's claim for reimbursement upon death by transferring them to irrevocable trusts. These trusts must be quite restrictive and are discussed in greater detail in Chapter 12.

Second, individuals can leave funds for their surviving spouse in testamentary trusts (see Chapter 3) that are much more flexible and protected from Medicaid spend down and estate recovery.

Third, the Medicaid law offers two safe harbors for people with disabilities who can transfer funds into trusts for their own benefit as long as Medicaid is reimbursed for its expenditures on their behalf from any funds remaining in trust when they pass away. These can be individual trusts, often referred to as "(d)(4)(A)" trusts, or they can be pooled trusts run by non-profit organizations, often referred to as "(d)(4)(C)" trusts (both names referring to the authorizing statute). These are discussed more fully in Chapter 13.

SHARED OWNERSHIP OF REAL ESTATE

Real estate ownership by multiple people who are not a married couple (and in some cases even when they are a married couple) raises a number of questions. Who is responsible for managing the property? Who can live there? What happens if money is needed for capital expenses? How should rental income be distributed? What happens if an owner becomes incapacitated or passes away?

These questions and others can be answered in a trust document, whether created by the current owners of the property or by parents or grandparents leaving property to future generations. In the second case, the trust can also provide liability protection for the beneficiaries of the trust. (Limited liability corporations are also used for liability protection and to define rights and obligations related to shared real estate ownership.)

MANAGEMENT OF VACATION PROPERTY FOR FAMILIES

Shared ownership of vacation homes is very similar to shared ownership of any real estate described above. But significant differences may include less concern that the benefits of the property be equally shared. Parents and grandparents creating a trust to hold a family vacation house may be more interested in making sure that it's available to any of their descendants who may want to make use of it than that they all share it equally. If that's the case, they need to create the structure that will allow this to happen, rather than simply leaving the property equally to their children, some of whom may have different ideas about their inheritance.

SHARED OWNERSHIP OF FAMILY BUSINESSES

Shared ownership of family businesses can get even more complicated than shared ownership of real estate. Who gets to (or has to) work in the business? How should they be compensated? Who should be rewarded for contributing to the growth of the business? Who should be in control? How should ownership be allocated?

These can be difficult questions, and the answers can lead to family resentments and even expensive legal disputes. (Those from Massachusetts may well remember the decades-long litigation over the ownership and control of the Market Basket supermarket chain.

The dispute got so heated that one lawyer was disbarred for trying to bribe a judge's law clerk to provide evidence to disqualify the judge from the case. Ultimately, when one side of the family dislodged the well-loved manager of the chain, both workers and customers went on strike, forcing a resolution of the dispute. As is usually the case in disputes, only the lawyers—the ones who were not disbarred—benefited from the saga.)

Clarity about plans and a clear structure for carrying them out can go a long way towards avoiding future disputes. Business owners often use limited liability corporations for this purpose, but the LLC shares are often owned by trusts.

PROVIDING FOR PETS AFTER DEATH

While traditionally only people and charities have been allowed to be beneficiaries of trusts, every state now permits pet owners to leave funds in trust for their pets. While many pet owners assume that they will outlive their pets or family members will simply adopt them, this is not the case if you don't have family members who can or will step into this role. And often it's individuals without children and grandchildren who are most attached to their pets. If you don't have a natural guardian for your pets and are asking for someone else to take on this role if necessary, it's important that they don't incur a financial burden for doing so. You can either leave the caregiver money directly in your estate plan or create a trust for this purpose. Having someone other than the person caring for the pet hold the purse strings can offer some assurance that the funds are spent as intended and will be available for a new caretaker if the first person cannot or will not fill this role for any reason.

SECOND MARRIAGES

Most second (or third or fourth) marriages or committed relationships need a prenuptial agreement as well as trusts. A first marriage may require a prenuptial agreement or trust if either party has significant assets or has children from a previous relationship. But in general, those getting remarried later in life are much more likely to have both children and assets. So, they need to answer questions such as these: Who gets what when they die? Does everything go to the new spouse? Or to the children? Or is a house for the new spouse for life only? What happens when the surviving spouse and children disagree? What happens when one spouse needs care in his later years?

These are questions that should be asked and answered before entering into a second marriage or even if you're in a committed long-term relationship. The financial terms of the relationship should be determined in advance and spelled out in a prenuptial or other written agreement. Whether or not a prenuptial agreement exists, in most cases trusts should be created to spell out how each spouse intends their assets be used if they become incapacitated or die before the other. They are ideal tools for taking care of the surviving spouse or partner while still making sure assets pass to children. This can be especially important if those assets were accumulated during a long marriage to the mother or father of those children.

CHAPTER 5

TRUSTEE RESPONSIBILITIES AND FIDUCIARY DUTY

If you are asked to serve as trustee, think it over before accepting. While it's a great honor to be selected, since it shows that the person asking has great faith in your abilities and probity, trustees have a lot of responsibilities and are held to a very high standard. It's best to read through this chapter before accepting the role.

The standard to which trustees are held is known as "fiduciary duty." Here's how it is defined in Wikipedia:

> A fiduciary duty is the highest standard of care in equity or law. A fiduciary is expected to be extremely loyal to the person to whom he owes the duty (the "principal") such that there must be no conflict

of duty between fiduciary and principal, and the fiduciary must not profit from their position as a fiduciary (unless the principal consents).

This means that a trustee must always put the beneficiaries' interests ahead of her own. She cannot self-deal, meaning she cannot use trust funds to invest in her own business or borrow money from the trust. If she is also a beneficiary, she may not favor herself over other beneficiaries.

This, of course, does not really come into play when you are trustee of your own revocable trust, since your fiduciary duty is to yourself. But if you are trustee of your own irrevocable trust, then it does come into play because you also have a duty to the other beneficiaries of the trust, even if their rights don't take effect until sometime in the future, even at your death.

In addition to self-dealing, one of the major breaches of fiduciary duty is neglect. If a trustee doesn't investigate the needs of beneficiaries or pay attention to investments, he may well be found to have neglected the trust and have violated his fiduciary duty. In contrast, a trustee who pays attention to the trust properties and beneficiaries will almost never be found to have neglected the trust, even if his decisions have turned out wrong.

For instance, a trustee will not be charged with losing a lot of money in investments even though they declined significantly during the COVID-19 downturn, as long as the trust fund was invested in a balanced portfolio and he had received the advice of professional financial advisors. On the other hand, a trustee who left all the funds in a money market account after the Great Recession and missed the huge increase in the market since then may well be found to have neglected the trust.

More specific trustee duties include investment, accounting, taxes, communication, and investigation.

INVESTMENT

Trust assets must be invested "prudently." This often means a mix of stocks and bonds, but some trusts also hold real estate, often a family home or vacation house. They may also hold interests in a family business or particular investment. Sometimes holding such interests might not be considered "prudent" as a strict investment matter, but other interests of the grantor or beneficiaries may outweigh investment decisions. For instance, if the trust holds the family home or a vacation property, the main purpose of the trust may be its preservation, in which case prudent investment concerns would hold little or no weight. This would also be the case if the trust held an interest in a family business. The trust itself may well include language either directing that the trust retain such property or investments, or relieving the trustee from liability for doing so.

Other than such unique holdings, trusts are held to the prudent investor standard, which, as is suggested above, involves a mix of bonds and stocks. Trusts generally invest conservatively, avoiding hedge funds or other higher risk investments, and diversify their stock investments. It would not be considered prudent to invest all their assets in stock, which could have devastated a trust portfolio in the COVID-19 downturn, or in bonds, which with recent low interest rates would mean that the trust holdings would lose value in relation to inflation. Typically, they would hold a balanced portfolio, with more or less invested in stocks depending on the ages and needs of the beneficiaries.

One example of how this might be done is my practice for a number of small trusts for which I serve as trustee because no other suitable trustee is available. I typically leave enough funds in a money market account to cover anticipated expenses for the coming year and invest the balance of funds as follows: 40% in a bond fund, 40% in a total U.S. stock market index fund, and 20% in an international stock market index fund. This approach provides stability and diversification at very low cost while permitting the trust funds to grow with the stock market.

ACCOUNTING

Trustees must keep meticulous records of trusts assets, income, expenses, and disbursements. Depending on the trust terms and state law, an account of such trust finances must be provided to beneficiaries on an annual basis or upon demand. This may be called an "account," "accounting," or "report," but whatever it's called, it means the same thing. Here's how this is described in the Uniform Trust Code, which has been adopted in 34 states (though any state may have modified this provision):

> A trustee shall send to the distributees or permissible
> distributees of trust income or principal, and to other
> qualified or nonqualified beneficiaries who request it,
> at least annually and at the termination of the trust,
> a report of the trust property, liabilities, receipts, and
> disbursements, including the source and amount of
> the trustee's compensation, a listing of the trust assets
> and, if feasible, their respective market values.

A "qualified" beneficiary is defined broadly as anyone to whom the trust currently might distribute income or principal, or who would be entitled to a distribution if the trust terminated or if a current qualified beneficiary's interest were to terminate. For instance, if a trust directed that the income be distributed to a mom for her life and then to her son, the son would be a qualified beneficiary as well as his mom. Again, your state may define this differently.

The level of detail of these accounts or "accountings" depends in part on the amount and nature of the assets in the trust and whether the trustee is a professional. At the very least, the trustee should be prepared to share financial statements for trust investments and those for trust operating accounts. For instance, if a trust owns rental property, the account should include all rental income, expenses for maintaining the property, and any distributions. Forwarding year-end statements for all trust accounts should do the trick for most trusts.

Professional trustees will prepare more formal accounts. Often these take a form similar to that required by probate courts for conservatorship and probate matters. These accountings state the total value of the trust assets at the beginning of the year (or other reporting period), funds coming in (whether interest and dividends or new contributions to the trust), funds going out (whether expenses or distributions), and the value of the trust fund at the end of the year. If the starting value plus incoming funds minus outgoing funds equals the ending value, then the account balances. Here's a simplified version of what this looks like:

Value of trust fund on January 1st	$100,000
Incoming funds	+$15,000
Disbursements and expenses	−$20,000
Value of trust fund on December 31st	$95,000

A complete accounting would list each of the investments held by the trust at the beginning and end of the accounting period, each item of incoming funds, and each expense or disbursement. An even more complete accounting would actually have two values for the beginning and end of the reporting period, showing the "book" value of each trust holding when purchased and their current market value. Testamentary trusts and other trusts that are under probate court jurisdiction must file these accountings with the court on an annual basis.

Traditionally, trusts had a third kind of trust accounting, which was even more complicated. They would keep separate income and principal accounts, in large part because trusts often had separate income and principal beneficiaries—for instance, one person might be entitled to the trust income during her life, with the balance distributed to other beneficiaries upon her death. What gets really complicated, in terms of understanding these account statements, is when there are transfers from the income account to the principal account. For instance, the trust may receive $183 in dividends for a certain investment. This will be recorded in the income account. Subsequently, the trustee may transfer $500 from the income side of the ledger to the principal side. This will be recorded as debit on the income accounting and an addition to the principal accounting, but the total value of the trust will remain the same. Many traditional trust companies—having the resources to purchase expensive trust accounting software—still use this form of accounting, and it may be required for some testamentary trusts where court reporting is required. (It also means that their accounting statements are very long.)

TAXES

For tax purposes, trusts are classified either as grantor trusts or non-grantor trusts. (Accountants also use the term "complex" trusts, but I have never found that to be a useful distinction.)

Revocable trusts are always grantor trusts and may use the grantor's Social Security number on trust accounts. Revocable trusts do not file their own tax returns since all trust income is reported to the grantor. But beware, when the grantor passes away, the trust will no longer be revocable even if its title still includes the word "revocable." If they don't end at the grantor's death, they are then irrevocable and like other irrevocable trusts must obtain their own tax identification number and file annual income tax returns using Form 1041.

Irrevocable trusts may or may not be grantor trusts and in fact can have split tax treatment, being treated as grantor trusts with respect to income and as non-grantor trusts with respect to principal. This can get quite complicated, and specific trust provisions—such as powers of appointment, the ability to change trustees, or the right to substitute property of equal value with trust property—may change the tax treatment of the trust. The significance is that income earned by a grantor trust will be taxed to the grantor and income earned by a non-grantor trust will be taxed to the grantor or other beneficiaries only to the extent it is distributed to them or used on their behalf.

Income retained by the trust will be taxed to the trust. This can result in higher taxes, because the tax rates for trust income are accelerated much more quickly than those for individuals, reaching the top bracket at just over $13,000 of income. Here are the current (2021) federal rates of taxation for trust income:

INCOME	RATE
$0 to $2,650	10%
$2,651 to $9,550	24%
$9,551 to $13,050	35%
Above $13,050	37%

As a general rule, irrevocable trusts that require all income to be distributed to the grantor will be taxed entirely to the grantor. There's some dispute as to whether the trust must obtain its own tax identification number (often called an "04" number) for such trusts, but it's certainly easier if the bank or financial institution will permit the trust account to use the grantor's Social Security number, since doing so avoids the need to file a separate trust tax return each year.

All non-grantor trusts must obtain a separate tax ID number and file a separate 1041 income tax return each year. But they may not pay taxes so long as they distribute their income to beneficiaries or use it on behalf of their beneficiaries. In addition, most trust expenses are deductible. To the extent trust income is distributed out, this is treated as a deduction on the trust return and the trust issues a K-1 to the beneficiary, who must report the income on his tax return. Here's an example of how this might work:

Trust's annual income	$15,000
Trust expenses	-$3,000
Trust distributions	-$9,000
Taxable income	$3,000

The trust in this example would issue a K-1 to the beneficiary for the $9,000 of income distributed; the beneficiary may or may not have to pay tax on it, depending on his other income. The trust would pay $349 in taxes [($2,650 x 0.10) + ($350 x 0.24)], considerably less than the approximately $2,775 it would pay without the pass through of income to the beneficiary. Of course, we don't know what taxes the trust beneficiary will pay on his $9,000 of trust income, but it's likely to be less than the trust would have paid with individual tax rates only reaching the 24% bracket in 2021 for income above $86,375 and the 35% bracket for income above $209,425.

In a variation on this example, let's assume the trust distributed $30,000 to the beneficiary instead of $9,000. While the beneficiary received $30,000 from the trust, $12,000 would have been from trust income and $18,000 from trust principal, with no tax reporting or payment necessary for the principal distribution. He would receive a K-1 showing $12,000 of income. The trust would have no taxable income after this deduction and pay no taxes.

If the trust assets are all held in a single account, the 1041 tax return is quite simple, since only one 1099 is involved. If the trust has many separate accounts or holds real estate or a business, the tax reporting can get more complicated. In either case, unless the trust is earning only interest income, it's better to have an accountant prepare the return to make sure it's done right. And, as an added benefit, the accountant's fee will be deductible.

COMMUNICATION

While it's vital that trustees communicate with trust beneficiaries, certain forms of communication are mandatory and some are simply good practice.

Mandatory communication can be a function of the trust document itself, which every trustee should read thoroughly and review regularly, or state trust law. As is discussed above, trustees must provide beneficiaries annual accounts of trust finances. In addition, under the Uniform Trust Code (which your state may or may not have adopted, and may or may not have modified) here are other instances when the trustee is required to give beneficiaries notice:

- Trustee resignations, removals, and appointments.
- The grantor's death.

- Trust amendments (though remainder beneficiaries of revocable trusts are not entitled to notice since their interests are never fixed until the grantor dies or the trust becomes irrevocable in some other fashion).

- Any judicial proceeding involving the trust.

- Termination of smaller trusts that are determined to be "uneconomic."

- Notice that a trust exists, which may be required when the beneficiary reaches the age of majority.

The Uniform Trust Code contains provision for waiver of certain notices and the ability to give notice to a representative of the beneficiary, for instance if the beneficiary is a minor or incapacitated.

Beyond these required forms of communication, trustees need to stay in touch with beneficiaries in order to understand their needs. A trustee is not simply an investment manager, even though that is one if her important functions. This is especially true if distributions are discretionary in nature rather than required. For instance, less knowledge of the beneficiary's circumstances is necessary if the trust requires distribution of income and bars distribution of principal than if it says either or both may be distributed as needed for the beneficiary's health and welfare. In the first instance, the trustee simply has to calculate the income and forward it to the beneficiary. In the second, the trustee must know and evaluate the beneficiary's health and welfare in order to determine what distributions are appropriate and necessary.

In addition to being available and responsive to beneficiaries when they reach out, it is good practice for trustees to seek out beneficiaries on a regular basis. In our practice, we contact all beneficiaries of trusts we manage at the beginning of each calendar year to schedule an annual meeting, whether in person, by video conference or on the telephone. This annual meeting may involve the beneficiary, other family members and advisors, such as accountants and investment managers. In the case of special needs trusts, it may involve health care professionals and care managers. These meetings make sure that we are aware of the beneficiary's circumstances and needs and allow us to adjust both disbursements and longer-range trust investment policy as appropriate.

It's good practice, in preparation for these annual meetings, for the trustee to review the trust to make sure she remembers its terms and can respond accurately to concerns or questions that are raised during the meeting.

We also have quarterly investment reviews with investment managers for trusts, though this usually does not include the beneficiaries. However, depending on the trust, the beneficiaries may have online access to review trust investments or receive copies of monthly or quarterly account statements, though they never have trading authority.

INVESTIGATION

In some instances, trustees need to go further than simple communication with beneficiaries and investigate their circumstances. In some cases this is because the beneficiaries don't respond or participate in annual meetings. Here are some potential examples:

- The beneficiary may receive or be eligible for certain public benefits. The trustee cannot simply pay for items or services that may be provided from other sources, thus unnecessarily depleting the trust fund for both current and future beneficiaries. In some cases, it's the trust distributions themselves that make the beneficiary ineligible for certain benefits. Where this may be the case, the trustee should investigate itself or engage professionals with knowledge in these fields.

- While the trustee cannot know everything going on in a beneficiary's life, there are instances that should give rise to suspicion that the beneficiary is being exploited and that trust distributions are going to someone other than the beneficiary. One marker of possible exploitation is when the trustee cannot reach the beneficiary or if someone else always responds purporting to represent the beneficiary. In these cases, the trustee needs to investigate to make sure that the distributions are actually going to the trust beneficiary.

- There are instances where trust beneficiaries live in dilapidated housing. While this is obviously a trust responsibility if the house or apartment is owned by the trust, it can also be a failure of trustee duty if trust money could be made available to fix the property or to provide adequate housing for the beneficiary. The trustee may need to visit the beneficiary or hire someone else to do so.

While every case is different, if the trustee maintains proper communication with beneficiaries as described above, she should be aware of circumstances where further investigation is necessary. The bottom line is that the trustee cannot blithely manage investments and distribute checks with no knowledge of the beneficiary's needs and the effect of such distributions.

CHAPTER 6
SPECIFIC TRUST TERMS

While every trust is different, many of their provisions may be similar or even "boilerplate." Here are the principal provisions that are anything but boilerplate and must be decided by the grantor in the case of almost all trusts:

RIGHTS TO INCOME AND PRINCIPAL

Every trust sets out the terms and conditions under which trust income (interest, dividends, rent) and principal are distributed. Distributions may be mandatory. For instance, the trust may require that income be distributed to one or more beneficiaries. Or it might be discretionary, permitting the trustee to determine when and for what purpose to make distributions. Or it may be discretionary within limits.

The trust may give the beneficiary the right to withdraw a certain amount of funds, whether at any time or on an annual basis.

Whatever the trust says, the trustee must know and follow the instructions.

DISTRIBUTION STANDARDS: DISCRETIONARY, LIMITED, FOR SPECIFIC PURPOSES

A common limitation on trustee discretion is to limit distributions to the beneficiary's health, education, maintenance, and support, the so-called HEMS standard. This might not seem like much of a limitation, and it isn't. But it does limit spending on luxuries or distributions for no purpose at all.

The reason the HEMS standard appears in many trusts is that it has significant tax implications. The limitation is sufficient, even if the trustee is also a beneficiary, to keep the trust property from being deemed to belong to the trustee for tax purposes. For instance, one spouse might leave a trust for the benefit of the other spouse who may also serve as trustee of his own trust. If he has complete discretion to use the trust property as he sees fit, it must be included in his estate when he dies (perhaps of little concern for federal purposes these days with the threshold set at $11.7 million (in 2021), but of more concern if he lives in a state with its own estate tax). However, if his ability to use the trust assets for his own benefit is limited by the HEMS standard (and he does not violate that standard) the trust assets will not be included in his estate when he dies.

Some courts (and others) have misinterpreted the HEMS standard as a requirement rather than a limitation. In other words, some courts have ruled erroneously that the trust funds must pay for the beneficiary's health, education, maintenance and support, when the standard actually dictates that the trustee may make distributions only for those items and nothing else—but doesn't have to. A trust can be written in such a fashion, but that is not how the HEMS standard is normally intended.

Trusts can be very creative and variable in how they direct trust distributions, including incentive trusts that pay out when the beneficiary has accomplished some goal, such as graduating from college or getting married. Here are some provisions I have seen (or drafted for clients):

- "Pot" trusts that hold a fund for all members of a generation to be used for their benefit as determined by the trustee. These often end when the youngest beneficiary reaches age 25, at which point the trust ends or it is divided into separate shares for the beneficiaries.

- Trusts that distribute when the beneficiaries reach certain ages, perhaps a third each at ages 25, 30, and 35.

- Payment(s)
    - for family vacations,
    - for a home, or just the down payment on a home,
    - to start a business,
    - matching a beneficiary's earnings, and/or
    - restricted to medical expenses.

POWER OF APPOINTMENT

A power of appointment gives someone the power to change who will receive trust property.

Often, grantors of irrevocable trusts keep the power to change who will receive the trust property after they pass away. With such a power they can maintain some control and respond to changing circumstances, whether to modify the trust terms because a child dies before them or a grandchild joins a cult. The power may also be given to others. For instance, a trust may be for the benefit of the grantor's children during their lives and give them the right to determine who will receive their various shares of the trust when the children pass away. This, hopefully, will be many decades after the grantor created the trust, when circumstances may have changed in a way the grantor could never anticipate. The power of appointment gives the next generation the ability to respond to such changing circumstances.

Most powers of appointment are "testamentary," meaning that they must be exercised in the will of the person with the power. This raises a bit of a contradiction since one benefit of the trust often is to avoid probate, but in order to put the power of appointment into effect, the will must be probated. Fortunately, such a probate can be efficient if its only purpose is to exercise the power and would not involve distributing property. In any case, powers of appointment generally are used as a safety hatch. The trust typically would provide for distribution of its property with the power of appointment being used only if necessary to change that distribution, similar to a switch changing which track a train will follow. So probating the will would only be necessary in the event such a switch needed to be used.

Less often, powers of appointment are *inter vivos*, meaning that they can be exercised during life. When they do appear in trusts, it's often for tax purposes, for instance to make the trust a grantor trust, without any intent that the power ever be used.

A more common distinction about powers of appointment is whether they are general or limited. A general power of appointment permits the power holder to appoint the trust property to any person or to any entity, such as a charity. Usually powers of appointment carry at least some limitation for tax and creditor protection purposes, barring distributions to the power holder's estate or creditors. Limited powers of appointment often require that trust funds remain in the family, limiting distributions to the grantor's children and grandchildren (or "issue") and in some cases their spouses. They also often permit distribution to charities.

Here's an example of limited power of appointment language in a trust:

> My surviving spouse shall have the limited power to appoint by Will all or any part of the principal of the Family Trust to the issue of myself by my spouse, or any of them, outright or in trust, in such proportions and amounts as my surviving spouse shall, in my surviving spouse's judgment determine, PROVIDED HOWEVER, that no exercise of such power shall be effective unless it shall make specific reference hereto.

RIGHT TO CHANGE TRUSTEES

In revocable trusts, the grantor can always hire and fire trustees at will, since she can always amend the trust. But after she dies or for irrevocable trusts, these powers need to be spelled out, giving them to a specific person or specific people, or to a class of people, such as the grantor's children.

Years ago, we represented a woman whose father had created a trust for her benefit naming the local bank as trustee. Since his death, the bank had been bought by a regional bank and then by a national bank, assigning our client to a young, nonresponsive trust officer located in another state. She wanted to change the trustee but didn't have the power to do so. She could have gone to court to seek the bank trustee's removal, but only "for cause," and it wasn't clear that bad communications or discomfort with the trustee were sufficient cause. In addition, she would have had to use her own funds to hire us to pursue the case while the bank could have dipped into the trust to defend its right to continue serving as trustee, probably hiring high-priced counsel from a downtown Boston law firm.

The Uniform Trust Code, fortunately, now supersedes the common law so that, in those states that have adopted it, beneficiaries no longer have to prove malfeasance by the trustee to get it replaced. The court may remove the trustee simply due to "a substantial change of circumstances or [if] removal is requested by all qualified beneficiaries [or] the court finds removal . . . serves the best interests of all the beneficiaries." Our client would have had a much easier time satisfying any of these requirements and would have had a much stronger position in convincing the bank to relinquish its role.

Our standard trust language permits the grantor to hire and fire trustees and in the grantor's absence gives the trustees this power. In other words, they can name their own replacements. If they can no longer serve, this power often passes to the grantor's descendants by generation, meaning his children can hire and fire trustees and, if none are alive and competent, then his grandchildren can do so.

This, of course, assumes that the grantor has children and grandchildren who can fill this role. If that isn't the case, this power may pass to named individuals or to a trust protector (as described in Chapter 2). In the event the person who has these powers is incapacitated, the trust may permit a guardian, conservator, or agent under a durable power of attorney to step in. Some trusts contain provisions permitting the law firm preparing the trust to name successor trustees. This can be a good fallback, though it can also be a bit self-serving if the firm itself is acting as trustee. If the trust has no provision for naming successor trustees or no one who has that power is alive and competent, ultimately it will be up to the local probate court to make these decisions.

A further question regarding hiring and firing trustees is whether there should be restrictions on who or what entity can serve as trustee. Provisions requiring that new trustees meet certain standards make sense. It could be very risky if a beneficiary could remove a trustee and name his best friend, neighbor, or lover to that role. Trusts often permit the grantor to name anyone as trustee but require that a trustee named by anyone else be independent and professional. A professional trustee may be an attorney, accountant, trust company, or bank. Sometimes trusts require institutional trustees and require that they be of a certain size, for instance that they have at least $100 million under management. Any of these requirements can make sure the person with the power to remove and appoint trustees does so with due consideration rather than making decisions in a casual or biased manner.

POWER TO REVIEW ACCOUNTS

While the Uniform Trust Code (UTC) requires the trustee to provide annual accounts to any current beneficiaries and any potential future beneficiaries who request accounts, the trust may provide others with the right to review accounts. It cannot, however, limit who has a right to receive accounts because this is one of the mandatory provisions in the UTC. Since the UTC provisions are quite broad, unless your state has narrowed them or you live in one of the 15 states that have not adopted the UTC, it's unlikely that the trust provisions will be broader except in one circumstance: The trust may require that annual accounts be provided to a trust protector in addition to beneficiaries.

The next question concerns what it means to "receive an account." Certainly sunlight is the best disinfectant, and the need to produce accounts will go a long way towards preventing trustee malfeasance or neglect. But what can the person receiving the account do if she disagrees with how the trust is being managed?

There's always a choice between informal advocacy—meeting with the trustee and explaining why, for instance, the trust funds should be invested differently or how the trust distributions can better meet the beneficiaries' needs—and more formal action such as changing trustees (if permitted under the terms of the trust) or going to court. Going to court should be avoided whenever possible, given its cost, the fact that the trustee can use trust funds to defend itself, and usually the burden of proof is on the person challenging the trustee actions. That said, sometimes beneficiaries have no other choice but to pursue a remedy in court.

It is important that those receiving trust accounts review them carefully and act promptly on any concerns they may raise because, pursuant to the UTC (which, again, may have been modified in your state), beneficiaries have one year after receiving a proper account to challenge the actions of trustees in court. Absent a proper accounting, the UTC has a very long statute of limitations: five years after (a) the trustee leaves its role for any reason, (b) the beneficiary's interest ends, or (c) the trust terminates. Since this could be a very long period, trustees have an incentive to satisfy beneficiary concerns in exchange for receiving a release from the beneficiaries.

CHAPTER 7
CHOICE OF TRUSTEE

Perhaps the most important and often difficult decision in creating a trust is whom to name as trustee or successor trustee.

In choosing a trustee, the considerations are somewhat different, depending on whether your trust is revocable or irrevocable. If you have a revocable trust, you will probably serve as its trustee, at least at first. But you should still name a successor trustee to serve in the event of your incapacity or if the trust will continue after your death. If your trust is irrevocable, whether created for tax planning, long-term care planning, special needs planning, or asset protection purposes, you will likely need a separate trustee from the outset.

Your main choice will be between a family member (or friend) and a professional trustee. Both have their advantages and potential disadvantages. A family member is likely to know you and your wishes better. You may feel more comfortable relying on a family member. And they probably won't charge for their services. However, a family member also may not do a good job of investing, keeping track of expenses, and communicating with other family members and beneficiaries. They may become distracted by their own life challenges or move to another part of the country or world.

A professional trustee, such as a bank, trust company, or attorney, may not know you well and may seem aloof. It will charge for its services. And it may be better or worse in terms of communication with you, family members, and other beneficiaries. On the other hand, it will provide continuity, handle investments professionally—if a bit conservatively—and take care of all the administrative duties, including trust accountings and tax returns.

These pros and cons are not the same for everyone, since both the family member and professional co-trustees available are different for each person. You may have very competent adult children who could step in and serve as your co-trustee or successor trustee as needed. And they may get along well with their siblings. You may have a close relationship with your local bank which has a good trust department or you may do all your banking online with no personal contact. Here are some of the issues you might consider in making your own choice:

- **Reliability.** Will your choice of trustee always be available to serve and respond to your needs and those of other beneficiaries?

- **Communication**. Will your trustee candidate communicate well with you and other beneficiaries?

- **Burden.** If considering a family-member trustee, will they be able to take on all the administrative chores of serving as trustee, including investments, annual accountings, paying bills, and filing tax returns?

- **Conflicts.** Conflicts can arise in two major ways. First, there can be a conflict of interest if the trustee is also a beneficiary, since distributions for or on behalf of some beneficiaries may reduce the interest of others. Conflicts can also arise— whether or not the trustee is also a beneficiary—if one or more beneficiaries disagree with the trustee's actions or decisions. Some beneficiaries may be more difficult personalities than others or the relationship between the beneficiary and the trustee may be difficult. For instance, you may not want to name one child as trustee of a special needs trust for the benefit of their brother or sister. It could be easier for all concerned if an independent third party served as trustee so that your children can simply be siblings.

- **Cost.** In most cases, a professional trustee will, on the surface, be more expensive than a non-professional trustee. Depending on the trustee and the size of the trust, the professional trustee may well charge a fee of 1.0% to 1.5% of the trust principal every year. Over time, this can add up. Nevertheless, it is usually money well spent. It makes certain that the trust is properly managed year after year, potentially saving the trust from poor investment and distribution decisions that can be much more costly than the fee. We have seen family-member trustees who are afraid to invest in the stock market and who missed the huge gain in stock prices after the Great Recession. We have also seen individuals lock in the coronavirus pandemic losses by fleeing the stock market after its more recent decline, rather than riding out its ups and downs. In that setting, daily swings in stock prices can far exceed costs of any professional trustee fees.

While you cannot be totally sure how a particular trustee choice will work out, here are a few strategies for optimizing your choice:

- **Testing.** Name your choice or choices of successor trustee as co-trustee now, while you're alive and healthy. This serves several purposes. You will see how your co-trustee acts in their role now and determine whether you think he or she should serve in this role on a long-term basis. By serving together, you and the trustee will get to know one another better and your co-trustee will have a better understanding of your situation, values and goals. And if you were to become incapacitated, your co-trustee would be in place to take over management of your finances as seamlessly as possible.

- **Trust Protector.** Whether someone has the formal title of "trust protector" or not, make sure your trust document gives one or more people the power to change trustees. No matter how carefully you plan, circumstances can change. Your local bank may be taken over by an international behemoth. Your trusted family member may fall ill. You need someone in place who can react to such changes.

- **Co-trustees.** Sometimes the best answer isn't either/or but both—both a non-professional and professional trustee. This permits the family member or friend who may best know the beneficiaries and their needs to stay involved, but includes a professional trustee to take care of all the administrative duties and to guide the family member on standard trust practices.

CHAPTER 8
TRUST FUNDING

One of the biggest gaps in terms of implementing estate plans is the failure to fund trusts. All too often, estate planning attorneys draft perfectly good trusts for clients and then don't guide them on how to fund their trusts or take the step to do this for them. This is important because trusts only control property that they own. They are totally irrelevant to property not titled in the name of the trust, unless you have a "pour over" will.

A "pour over" will simply says that any property in your estate not specifically directed to particular people will pass to your trust. They are usually included in estate plans designed around revocable trusts to make sure nothing falls through the cracks. But the idea is that they won't be used, since one of the purposes of revocable trusts is to avoid probate and the need for any will at all.

On two occasions in our practice we've had estates involving men who created their trusts on their own and didn't execute wills or fund the trusts. The result in one case was that the property went to people the man had intended to disinherit. In the other, the man's quite honorable children agreed to follow their father's wishes even though this meant giving his $1 million house to his girlfriend.

Some trusts include an appendix listing the assets to be placed in them. Other than tangible personal assets, such as furniture, artwork and silverware, these should not be relied on. Instead, you must take the affirmative step of retitling your property into trust. Here's how to do so:

BANK AND INVESTMENT ACCOUNTS

To place bank and investment accounts into your trust, you need to retitle them in the names of the trustees as follows:

> Michelle and Barack as Trustees of The Michelle Revocable Trust created by agreement dated June 26, 2017.

Depending on the institution, you may be able to change the name on an existing account or they will require you to open a new account in the name of the trust and then transfer the funds. The financial institution will probably require a copy of the trust, or at least of the first page and the signature page, as well as signatures of all the trustees.

If the trust is revocable, you can use your own Social Security number for the trust accounts. However, if it is irrevocable you will have to obtain a tax identification number for the trust and file an annual income tax return.

Often funding trusts serves as an opportunity to consolidate investments that have accumulated over the years in many different financial institutions. Doing so can go a long way towards getting a better picture of your financial situation, which can lead to better financial planning and make the task of administering your estate much easier for your heirs.

REAL ESTATE

To transfer real estate, you must sign both a new deed conveying the property into the trust and a trustee's certificate certifying to the basic information about the trust, including:

- its name,

- the date it was created,

- the identity of both current and successor trustees, and

- its address.

Both the deed and the trustee's certificate must be notarized.

If you have a mortgage on your property, the mortgage document probably contains a provision requiring notice of any change in title and perhaps even a due-on-sale clause that applies transfers into trusts. However, we have never given notice in our practice and have never seen an issue arise, as long as the clients continue to make their monthly mortgage or line of credit payments. However, if you intend to refinance your property or take out a line of credit, wait until you do so before deeding the real estate into your trust. In most instances, banks and other lenders require that you remove the property from the trust and put it back in your name before signing any new mortgage papers.

RETIREMENT PLANS

You cannot retitle your IRA or 401(k) in the name of your trust. That would force a liquidation of the account and the payment of taxes on it, which you don't want. In addition, you may or may not want to name your trust as beneficiary of your IRA. If your trust ends at your death with everything being distributed to your beneficiaries, it's easier simply to name them as beneficiaries of the IRA. On the other hand, if your trust will continue after your death to provide for management and protection of the trust assets for your beneficiaries, then you can provide these same protections to your IRA funds by naming the trust as the beneficiary at your death.

However, before you take this step make sure that the trust meets the requirements to qualify as a designated beneficiary so that the minimum distributions can be stretched out, depending on the beneficiary, either over her entire life or over the 10 years following your death. If the trust does not meet these requirements, the IRA will have to be liquidated within five years of your death and all of the taxes paid on it at that time. This is explained in more detail in Chapter 18. It can get pretty complicated; your estate planning attorney should be able to advise you on the options available.

VEHICLES

Depending on your state, you may or may not be able to title your car or other vehicle in the trust. If not, the pour-over provision in your will can make sure it goes to the right person upon your death. This may require that your will be probated, but there's usually an expedited process for doing so if the estate is small or holds only a vehicle. Some states even have special rules for vehicles, especially if they're passing to a spouse.

DON'T FORGET BENEFICIARY DESIGNATIONS

Finally, make sure that you update the beneficiary designations for your insurance policies and for any accounts that permit named beneficiaries so that they name the trust. Otherwise, you could have inconsistencies in your estate plan with your trust saying one thing and your other accounts saying something else. This can lead to confusion, resentments and even litigation. Make sure your entire plan is consistent. However, do not name the trust as beneficiary of your retirement accounts without first consulting with an estate planning professional (see above).

CHAPTER 9
TRUSTEE COMPENSATION

Trustees are entitled to "reasonable" compensation whether or not the trust explicitly provides for such.

PROFESSIONAL TRUSTEES

Typically, professional trustees—such as banks, trust companies, and some law firms—charge between 1.0% and 1.5% of trust assets per year, depending in part on the size of the trust. They charge a higher percentage for smaller trusts, typically under $1 million, and less for larger trusts, typically over $2 million, since the amount of work involved is more or less the same no matter the size of the trust.

In the past, professional trustees would often charge both a percentage of the trust principal and a percentage of the trust's annual income, in part because trusts often provide that the income and principal beneficiaries are different. For instance, a trust might provide that the income be paid to a surviving spouse but that the principal be preserved to pass on to the children upon the spouse's death. If the fee came solely from the trust principal, it would seem that the surviving spouse would be getting a free ride, since her income stream would not share the expense (except secondarily to the extent the trust income declined due to the slightly lower trust principal resulting from the trustee fees). In recent years, with the decline in trust income due to chronically low interest rates, it has become customary to charge the fee only to trust principal.

While percentage fees are standard, they can be problematic for smaller trusts. A trust holding $200,000 with a 1.5% fee would pay $3,000 annually, which may or may not cover the trustee's costs. Some professional trustees charge a minimum of $5,000 a year, meaning the effective rate for such a smaller trust would be 2.5% a year, which could erode the value of the trust over time. In my own practice where we end up being trustees of last resort for a number of smaller trusts—cases where there's no appropriate person in the family to act as trustee and the trust is too small to engage a traditional bank or trust company—we charge our standard hourly rates for our work plus 0.5% per year. For a trust holding $200,000, for instance, this would entail an extra charge of $1,000 a year. The total annual fees may be more or less than the $5,000 standard minimum, depending on the amount of work involved, but in most cases is substantially less.

Survey results published online by Wealth Advisor (https://www. thewealthadvisor.com/article/whos-charging-what-trust-services) report the fees charged by national trust companies, which are consistent with the information above. Annual fees range from 0.5%

to 1.0% of trust assets up to $1 million, with minimum fees ranging from $100 to $8,000, with most in the $3,000 range. For the most part, these fees seem not to include investment management, which would then be an additional cost. The trust company with the $8,000 minimum fee is undoubtedly trying to discourage smaller trusts from using its service.

NON-PROFESSIONAL TRUSTEES

Fees are less standard when a non-professional acts as trustee, either on her own or in conjunction with a professional trustee. Where the professional trustee is doing most of the heavy lifting, many non-professional trustees, who are often family members, take no fee. However, just as often they do take a fee, especially if they are not a close family member of the grantor, for instance if they are a niece or nephew. The standard I've seen is 0.25%, which on a trust holding $1 million would be $2,500 a year. Where there's no professional trustee acting, the non-professional trustee can certainly charge a higher fee and can use the professional standards as a guide. However, they should look at other trust costs. For instance, professional trustees usually take care of the investments as part of their function. If the trust is hiring an investment advisor, that cost should be considered in determining the trustee's fee so that together they don't get too high.

Difficulties can arise when a family member or friend trustee's fees are not clear. Some trustees assume they can charge for their time, which may be appropriate, but probably not at the rate they charge for what they do professionally. In addition, sometimes family members are not very efficient and, as a result, take a lot of time that may not seem necessary to the beneficiaries. It can prove more cost effective and less controversial to hire others to carry out necessary functions, whether that's cleaning out a house owned by the trust or accounting for trust income, investments, and expenditures. Then there's a clear distinction between the trust expense and the trustee fee.

Often family members don't charge anything for many years and then seek to be paid in arrears for many years of service. This can create resentments when the beneficiaries do not anticipate having to pay fees and the total becomes a large sum.

The best solution is transparency and consistency. If anyone being asked to serve as trustee expects or hopes for compensation, she should discuss this with the grantor and arrive at an agreement about what is appropriate. If that discussion did not happen, the trustee should have the same discussion with the trust beneficiaries. The agreement should be put in writing. Even an email confirmation will do the trick. Fees should be paid on an annual basis if possible. If not possible, for instance if the only trust asset is nonproductive real estate, then the trustee should make it clear to the beneficiaries what fees may be accumulating. It could come as a big surprise to the beneficiaries if, after 20 years of managing a $500,000 property, on its sale the trustee seeks a $100,000 fee.

Finally, trustees need to understand that trustee fees constitute taxable income and must be reported on their tax returns.

SECTION 2
LET'S GET SPECIFIC

CHAPTER 10
REVOCABLE TRUSTS

Essentially, a revocable trust is a new financial entity that you create. As the creator, you are called the "grantor" or the "donor." You are also at least one of the beneficiaries of the trust and can serve as the sole trustee or as one of a number of co-trustees, or you can name other individuals or institutions as trustees. The trustees manage the assets in the trust, which can include real estate, bank accounts, investments and tangible property, such as fine art, under the terms set forth in the trust document. In principle, a trust document can be as short as this:

> I, Michelle, hereby create this trust as grantor and trustee. If I ever become incapacitated or upon my death, my husband, Barack, will step in as trustee. During my life, the trustee may distribute principal

and income to me or on my behalf as the trustee in its sole judgment determines appropriate. After my death, all the remaining income and principal shall be distributed to my good friend, Joe. I may amend or revoke this trust at any time by delivering a writing signed by me to any trustee.

Michelle

While Michelle fills all three roles—grantor, trustee and beneficiary—today, she is not the sole beneficiary, since Joe will get the trust funds when she dies. As a result, she can manage the trust property as if it were still titled in her name, even using her own Social Security number on trust bank and investment accounts. The purpose of the trust is to avoid probate, provide for management of the trust assets upon Michelle's incapacity, and govern how they will be held in continuing trust or distributed upon Michelle's death.

PROBATE AVOIDANCE

Over my decades of practice, I have become a strong proponent of revocable trusts as a means to avoid probate and, more importantly, to provide for asset management in the event of incapacity. Probate avoidance has been the argument for revocable trusts, sometimes marketed as "living" trusts or even "loving" trusts, that lawyers have used for decades, often with horror stories about how cumbersome and expensive the probate process can be for heirs. While dealing with the probate court can add some burden to the process of passing on possessions at one's death, it's usually not as difficult or time consuming as the horror stories would indicate. In addition, avoiding the probate courts does not mean that all the executor or personal representative's duties can be avoided. She must still collect and distribute the decedent's assets, clean out any apartment or house, pay last debts, and file final tax returns, among other tasks.

That said, the revocable trust does have significant benefits upon the grantor's death. Simply the act of funding the trust often prompts the grantor to clean up her financial life, consolidating her investments and savings at a single institution. This upfront work can save the executor a lot of work and time down the road. Since the successor trustee or co-trustee can step into his role without first seeking court appointment, he can take control of assets, pay bills, and make distributions to beneficiaries much more easily. However, the trust only avoids probate to the extent it is funded. Any property not transferred to the trust, in joint names, or having a beneficiary designation will still have to be probated.

As I write this, I am trustee and personal representative for a woman who recently died. Her trust holds approximately $530,000 and her bank account approximately $140,000. I liquidated and distributed the bulk of the trust assets to the beneficiaries within a couple of weeks (distributing $250,000 each to the decedent's brother and sister, while holding back the balance for any future expenses, such as the final trust income tax return). But I can't touch my client's bank account until I'm appointed by the court, which could take more than a month and will require a trip to the bank.

So, probate avoidance is a definite benefit of revocable trusts. Of course, it must be balanced against the cost of setting up the trust, including upfront legal fees and the effort the grantor must take to transfer ownership of assets to the trust. Further, if the grantor owns real estate and needs to tap into the equity or refinance, banks will not extend new mortgages or home equity lines of credit to property in trust. The grantor may well have to transfer the property out of the trust to get the loan, and then execute a new deed transferring it back into the trust after the loan has been secured, a somewhat expensive and bothersome process.

In states that still have an estate tax, revocable trusts are often used for estate tax planning, which is discussed in Chapter 11. They're also important for planning for minor children, which is discussed below in this chapter. However, a main purpose of revocable trusts, which in my mind breaks any tie between the cost and burden of setting up the trust and the cost and burden of probate, is their usefulness in the event the grantor becomes incapacitated.

INCAPACITY

With respect to Michelle's trust above, in the event of incapacity, Barack can step in and manage the trust property without any fuss. While he might also do so through a durable power of attorney, we have found that banks and other financial institutions are much more comfortable with trusts. They have been known to reject durable powers of attorney that are more than a few years old or to require that the drafting attorney certify that the power of attorney has not been revoked. (This puts the attorney in an awkward position, since he cannot really know what the client did in his absence, but he'll usually sign the affidavit to help out the client's family.)

Especially with older clients who are more likely to become incapacitated or be the victims of scams aimed at seniors, we recommend that they appoint co-trustees in addition to successor trustees. If Michelle were to follow this advice, she would name Barack as her co-trustee and Melia as successor trustee. Barack's appointment as co-trustee would make his ability to step in in the event of Michelle's incapacity or death entirely seamless. Since he would already be on the accounts, he would not have to take any steps to prove Michelle's incapacity and sign on to the accounts or other property.

Seniors are common targets of scams. They often have accumulated savings, they may be vulnerable, not having the cognitive strength they may have had when younger, and often they are isolated. Having a co-trustee can offer useful protection. The senior can continue to manage her accounts, pay her bills, and manage her investments. But the co-trustee can keep an eye on accounts online and step in if she sees any unusual activity.

POST-DEATH PLANNING

The revocable trust can simply end upon the grantor's death or it can continue, providing investment management, tax minimization and asset protection for future generations. Revocable trusts are often used for all the purposes irrevocable trusts may be used: to shelter assets from estate taxation, creditors and divorce; to make sure they stay in the family when a spouse or children die; to provide for fund management for minor children or grandchildren; and/or to permit an heir with special needs to maintain eligibility for public benefits.

Interestingly, the names of revocable trusts that continue after the death of the grantor can be a bit confusing since at that point they become irrevocable. If Chelsea is the beneficiary of The Hillary Rodham Revocable Trust after Hillary's death, can she revoke or amend it? Usually not. To avoid this confusion we've stopped using the word "revocable" in revocable trusts created in our office. Hillary's trust would simply be called The Hillary Rodham Trust, making it clearer to Chelsea that she must abide by whatever terms Hillary chose for the trust.

CHAPTER 11
ESTATE TAX PLANNING

Trusts are principal tools for estate tax planning to remove property from an individual's taxable estate. Revocable trusts are used to keep the assets of the first spouse to die out of the taxable estate of the surviving spouse. Irrevocable trusts may be used to remove property from an individual's estate during life, often holding life insurance policies, or to keep property passing to a future generation outside of that generation's taxable estates. These last trusts are sometimes called "generation-skipping" trusts, as described below.

With the federal estate tax threshold set at $11.7 million per individual and $23.4 million for married couples (in 2021), very few people have to worry about estate taxes. But the threshold is much lower for estate taxes in some states, and the federal threshold is slated to drop by half on January 1, 2026. So this brings in a few more people who might be concerned about estate tax planning.

REVOCABLE TRUSTS AND SPOUSAL PLANNING

A very typical form of estate planning for married couples with taxable estates, either under their state's laws or federally, is for each spouse to create and fund a revocable trust that will provide for the surviving spouse after the first spouse passes away, but not be included in the surviving spouse's estate. Here's how this would work in my state of Massachusetts, which has a $1 million estate tax threshold.

Let's assume that Mr. and Mrs. Smith together own property and investments worth $2 million. Let's also assume that Mr. Smith passes away first and that at Mrs. Smith's death, she'll still have $2 million. If they engage in no estate tax planning, there will be no estate tax upon Mr. Smith's death because in Massachusetts (as well as federally) there's no tax on property passing to your spouse. (It was this rule that doomed the federal ban on same-sex marriages since the surviving spouse in the case claiming discrimination had to pay an estate tax because the federal government didn't recognize her marriage. The Supreme Court found this to be discriminatory.) However, with $2 million still in her name at her death, Mrs. Smith's estate would have a tax of about $100,000—not confiscatory, but totally avoidable through estate tax planning.

Under the standard plan, both Mr. and Mrs. Smith would each execute revocable trusts and divide their assets between them, each funded with $1 million. They would both do this because we can't know which will die first, though in our example it's Mr. Smith. At his death, his trust would continue for Mrs. Smith's benefit, with the trust designed to exclude its holdings from Mrs. Smith's taxable estate. Even if it grows in value during Mrs. Smith's life to total well more than $1 million at her death, it still won't be taxed.

It's possible that Mr. and Mrs. Smith's assets grow to more than $2 million before Mr. Smith passes away. To account for this or in case they already have more than $2 million, trusts are drafted in one of two ways.

Credit shelter trusts

The first is for the trust to contain two separate subtrusts: a credit shelter trust and a marital trust. While the language can get a little complicated to account for variations on how property is held, the simplest explanation is that, in the case of Massachusetts, the first $1 million—the estate tax credit—goes into the credit shelter trust. Any excess goes into the marital trust (or in some cases outright to the surviving spouse).

The surviving spouse typically has free access to the marital trust, since those assets will be counted in her taxable estate in any case, but somewhat limited access to those assets in the credit shelter trust. If there's an independent trustee, discretion to make distributions may be left to it. If the surviving spouse is the sole trustee, typically the limitation on principal distributions refers to the so-called "ascertainable" or "HEMS" standard permitted under the IRS rules. The magic words are that the principal may be distributed to the surviving spouse only for her "health, education, maintenance, and support." It's not much of a limitation, but presumably it wouldn't cover a yacht or a Rolls Royce. In any case, it's usually a better idea for the surviving spouse to spend her own funds and funds in the marital trust before those in the credit shelter trust since they would be taxable upon her death and those in the credit shelter trust would not be, no matter how much they grew over time.

QTIP trusts

The second design or type of trusts for surviving spouses is known as "QTIP," which stands for "qualified terminable interest property" (but you can forget that immediately since everyone just calls them "QTIP" trusts). These trusts permit the surviving spouse to choose (or in estate planners' parlance "elect") how to treat the trust funds, whether they end up in her taxable estate or not. She can split the funds into two shares, depending on which treatment will bring the best tax outcome, taking into account capital gains as well as estate taxes. (Back in the days when the federal estate tax threshold was much lower, the surviving spouse might divide the trust property into three shares with different shares receiving different state and federal tax treatment.)

To qualify as a QTIP, the trust simply must provide that all income earned be distributed to the surviving spouse and it must not give her complete access to the principal. In terms of principal distributions, the trust can be structured in either of the ways described above for the marital trust—discretion up to an independent trustee or use of the HEMS standard—or principal distributions can be entirely barred. The latter option might be used in the case of a second marriage where the decedent wants the surviving spouse to have funds to live on, but to retain the corpus for her family.

The QTIP option may be structured as a single trust for the surviving spouse, or the two-trust model described above may be used with the marital share drafted as a QTIP trust.

Portability

While credit shelter and QTIP trusts have long been used for estate tax planning at the state and federal levels, passage of portability in

2010 allowed surviving spouses to protect the unused portion of their deceased spouse's estate tax exemption simply by filing a federal estate tax return for the surviving spouse. That way the surviving spouse can, in effect, double her estate tax exemption without needing to use a QTIP or credit shelter trust.

For example, if one spouse dies with an estate valued at $4 million, the remaining $7.7 million of the $11.7 million exemption (in 2021) is "portable" to the remaining spouse, but only if they file a estate tax return and elect portablity. Then the surviving spouse will have a total federal estate tax exemption of $19.4 million ($7.7 million + $11.7 million) upon their death.

QTIP and credit shelter trusts still offer state tax protection and creditor protection, as well as protecting the children of the first spouse to die, but portability has rendered them necessary for only the very wealthy under the current estate tax exemption. When federal estate tax exemptions expire in 2026, these trusts will again apply to more "merely wealthy" individuals.

Powers of appointment

One issue to consider in drafting a spousal trust for estate tax planning is whether to give a surviving spouse a power of appointment and, if so, how broad it should be. A power of appointment offers important flexibility for the surviving spouse to redirect where trust funds will go at her death, which can be important in order to respond to changes in circumstances. You may not want your daughter in the middle of a divorce to inherit funds or for them to go to a grandchild who is facing challenges with drug addiction. On the other hand, you might not want to give your spouse the right to have the trust funds pass to his new spouse or lover, so you might limit the power to reallocate trust proceeds to your children and grandchildren or to trusts on their behalf.

You should especially take a look at the power of appointment if you're in a second marriage. In a case in Massachusetts, a surviving second spouse used her power of appointment to direct that the funds in trust left by her deceased husband go to her children instead of to his. His children brought a claim against the estate planning attorney, arguing that giving her this power was malpractice. No doubt, the broad power of appointment was simply a boilerplate provision in the lawyer's documents because most of his clients were not in second marriages with two separate sets of offspring. But the children lost their case because they had the burden of proving that this was not what their father wanted and had no real evidence to overcome that burden.

GENERATION-SKIPPING TRUSTS

Just as an individual can leave funds for her surviving spouse that can be spent for his benefit and not be included as taxable in his estate when he dies, parents and grandparents can leave funds in trust for their children and grandchildren that will not be taxed when the children and grandchildren pass away. As with many estate tax planning strategies, the benefit of these trusts was much greater when the estate tax threshold was much lower and many more estates were subject to federal estate taxation. These "generation-skipping trusts" also have significant creditor and divorce protection benefits, which are described in Chapter 15 on Family Protection Trusts.

In essence, just like the marital trust described above, to keep the funds in trust out of the next generation's taxable estate, it must limit principal distributions. Again, this can be done by giving control over such distributions to an independent trustee or limiting them to the HEMS standard. This can continue for as many generations as the parent or grandparent chooses, but typically at some point the trust ends and at the death of the last survivor of one generation, with the remaining principal distributed to the members of the subsequent generation. Under the common law, trusts have to satisfy the "rule against perpetuities," which has bedeviled the lives of first-year law students for centuries. In essence, it requires that all trusts end within 21 years after the death of the last beneficiary who was alive (what the common law calls a "life in being") upon the creation of the trust or when it became irrevocable. More recently, some states have moved to eliminate the rule against perpetuities and permitted the creation of so called "dynasty" trusts that might last up to 1,000 years. Personally, I think that's a bad idea. Does it make any sense for people today to be governed by an instrument written in 1620? Who knows what the world will look like in 2420, or beyond?

But back to generation-skipping trusts. In reaction to their creation as a common estate tax planning tool, Congress created a limitation on how much could be protected from taxation upon the death of the next generation through the generation-skipping tax. This is very complicated and of no relevance to anyone who has less than $11.7 million in 2021 (or about half that amount when the latest increase in the estate and generation-skipping taxes reverts in 2026 back to the tax in place before the Ryan-Trump tax cuts of 2017). If your estate is that large, you need estate tax planning advice from an expert.

LIFE INSURANCE TRUSTS

Another estate tax planning device that was common when the estate tax threshold was lower and is much less common today is the life insurance trust. These trusts permit the creation of a large pool of funds for their family that will not be subject to estate tax and will leverage the annual $15,000 (in 2021) that taxpayers can give to any number of beneficiaries without having to file a federal gift tax return.

Here's how this works. The client creates an irrevocable trust for the benefit of her family and names someone independent as trustee. The trust then buys a life insurance policy on the client's life. At the client's death, the life insurance policy pays out free of both estate and income taxes. At that point the trust can end or continue for the benefit of the client's heirs, depending on what she chooses. If she has a surviving spouse, she may want the trust to continue during the spouse's life so that it's not taxable at the spouse's death.

The tricky part has to do with coming up with the funds to pay the insurance policy premiums. Transfers of funds into trust typically do not qualify for the $15,000-per-year gift tax exclusion because trusts are not people for purposes of the annual gift tax exclusion (even if the Supreme Court thinks corporations are people for purposes of the first amendment). So, one option is for the client to file a gift tax return whenever she transfers funds to the trust to pay the premiums. This will work, but each such filing reduces the amount that she can give away tax free at death. As with much of estate tax planning, this was a bigger issue when the threshold was $1 million or less than it is today with the threshold at $11.7 million.

Instead of using up one's estate tax credit, a workaround has been established known as the "Crummey" power, named after a case of that name. Crummey powers require that the trust beneficiaries be notified of any contribution to the trust and that they have a certain amount of time, usually 30 days, within which to withdraw the contributed funds. That right of withdrawal is sufficient for the contribution to the trust to be treated as a gift to an individual and to qualify for the $15,000 annual gift tax exclusion. Of course, beneficiaries almost never exercise their rights of withdrawal since doing so could well undermine the purpose of the trust as well as the prospect of getting further gifts from the trust donor.

The problem with Crummey powers is that it's rather a pain to follow the rules. Donors and non-professional trustees often fail to do so. Larger law firms that administer many life insurance trusts can establish staffing and procedures to handle these for their clients. Smaller firms that only have a few such trusts can find it difficult to track them and difficult to charge a fee for doing so commensurate with the work and responsibility involved.

Given that today, federally, there's no need for a life insurance trust unless your estate exceeds $11.7 million for an individual and $23.4 million for a couple, life insurance trusts are being created only by the mega-wealthy. However, with the thresholds slated to be cut in half in 2026, they may be of interest to the merely wealthy as well. If you fall in that category, you may want to act now rather than waiting until 2026 since your insurability may change in the meantime. Just speaking for myself, I've been going to see specialists for various ailments and conditions a lot more since turning 60 than before, which might affect my insurability. (Actually, I never went before.)

TRUSTS WE'RE ONLY GOING TO MENTION

There are several other kinds of trusts used in estate tax planning that are beyond the scope of this ebook, including QPRTs and charitable remainder trusts.

QPRTs

"QPRT" stands for qualified personal residence trust. These are used to remove valuable real estate from a taxpayer's estate while permitting him to continue to live in it for the rest of his life through a lease. This way both the real estate and the rental payments are removed from his estate. The drawback of QPRTs is that while they can significantly reduce estate taxes for very large estates, if the heirs sell the real estate they may well be subject to higher capital gains taxes. This is not an issue if they don't sell the property and, with roughly a 20% differential between the federal estate and capital gains tax rates, it can still be a wise plan—but only for those who have taxable estates.

Charitable remainder trusts

Charitable remainder trusts, in effect, provide donors with two charitable deductions: an income tax deduction for contributions to the trust plus the removal of the gifted property from the donor's taxable estate. Since the benefit of the income tax deduction is not restricted to people with taxable estates, charitable remainder trusts can be of benefit to donors with smaller estates, but only if they have sufficient other deductions to itemize.

Typically, charitable remainder trusts provide that during the donor's lifetime the trust income or a certain percentage of trust assets be distributed to the donor during his life. At his death, the trust principal is distributed to one or more charities. These charities can be named in the trust but may be subject to change by the donor or the trustee. In some cases, the income stream continues for another generation before the trust corpus is distributed.

Since the donor retains an interest in the transferred property or funds, he can't take an income tax deduction on the full value of such property. Instead, for tax purposes the value is discounted based on the nature of the retained interest. The higher the annual payment and the younger the donor (assuming the trust only continues for his life), the greater the discount because the retained value is higher. Accountants and tax attorneys can provide the calculation in any individual case.

Charitable remainder trusts are often used by taxpayers with highly appreciated real estate. They may want to sell the property but are deterred by the tax they'll have to pay on the capital gains. If they first transfer such property to a charitable remainder trust and the trust sells the property, it does not have to pay any tax on the capital gain because it is treated as a charity. The donor then can receive the income produced by the total proceeds for the rest of his life, rather than from just what's left after paying the taxes on the capital gain.

Both QPRTs and charitable remainder trusts are quite technical, both in their execution and in calculating the costs and benefits. Anyone considering them needs to consult with experts who have experience with these planning strategies.

CHAPTER 12
MEDICAID PLANNING

In the United States, long-term care—whether at home, in assisted living, or in a nursing home—is not covered by health insurance or Medicare. Only about one in ten older Americans has long-term care insurance. As a result, while most care is provided by family members at no charge, when care by others is needed it is paid for out-of-pocket or through Medicaid, the health care safety net for the poor. Medicaid's eligibility rules are extremely complicated and can differ from state to state, since each state operates its own Medicaid program, but they are all similar. It's the details that can be different and can trip up the uninitiated.

Older Americans can spend down their funds when they need care, qualifying for Medicaid when they run out of their own resources, or they can plan ahead to qualify for Medicaid while still protecting assets for their spouse, children, or other heirs. Several kinds of trusts may be used for both advance and crisis (when the need for care arises) planning. What follows will not be an exhaustive description of Medicaid-planning techniques (because that could be a book in its own right), but instead an introduction to the different types of trusts used in Medicaid planning. Anyone doing Medicaid planning is advised to consult with a qualified elder law attorney due to both the complicated nature of such planning and the local differences in the rules and their application.

IRREVOCABLE TRUSTS

Under the Medicaid eligibility rules in most states, applicants may have only $2,000 in countable assets and their spouses about $129,000 (this figure increases with inflation each year). All savings and investments are counted against these limits as well as retirement plans in most states. Personal residences are not counted except to the extent their equity exceeds $838,000 (a figure that is adjusted each year for inflation and which may be lower in some states).

With respect to homes, I often say that Medicaid doesn't get you coming, it gets you going. This is because while you can keep your home and get Medicaid coverage, after your death the state Medicaid agency has the right to recover its costs paid out for your care from your estate, and the only substantial asset likely to be in your estate will be your home.

An irrevocable trust can be used to protect your home from such "estate recovery" and protect other assets from having to be spent down before you become eligible for Medicaid coverage.

Before we go any further, you need to know two other Medicaid rules. First, the transfer of funds or property into an irrevocable trust can cause you to be ineligible for Medicaid coverage for the subsequent five years. This is known as the "transfer penalty," because of the penalty of being ineligible due to the transfer for up to five years, or as the "look-back period," because when you apply for Medicaid you must report all transfers made during the prior five years. You do not need to report any transfers you may have made more than five years before applying for Medicaid benefits. (In some circumstances, the transfer penalty can be shorter than five years, but that gets complicated and is beyond the scope of this discussion. It's best to just think of any transfer as causing five years of ineligibility for benefits.)

The second rule is that if you are the beneficiary of any trust that you or your spouse created and funded, the assets in that trust will be considered available to you to the extent the trustee has discretion to distribute such assets to you or your spouse. As a result, irrevocable trusts used in Medicaid planning should be thought of as lock boxes. What you put in, you can't take out. For this reason, they're used more to protect family homes than other assets. Clients often want to protect their homes for their families and are less concerned about protecting their savings and investments, which are meant to be available for the rainy day in any case. (This is reflected in an academic report I heard presented recently in which the researchers asked why more seniors don't dip into the equity in their homes to pay for their living and care needs. The answer they found is that they want to preserve their homes to pass on to their heirs.)

When considering putting your home into an irrevocable trust, understand that you will not be able to take it out again. You also won't be able to take out the equity through a line of credit or reverse mortgage on the home. The trustees could, however, sell the house and buy another place for you to live. If you might rent out the house and depend on the income, the trust should provide that such income be payable to you. For this reason, these trusts are sometimes referred to as "income-only" trusts since you can only take out the income.

When considering putting savings and investments into an irrevocable trust, make sure you keep out enough funds to cover your needs for the five-year penalty period in case you need care during that time (or roll the dice, but understand that that's what you're doing). You can't put retirement funds in an irrevocable trust (or a revocable one for that matter) without first withdrawing them and paying taxes on the resulting income. As with a trust holding real estate, you can use an income-only trust so that you continue to receive any interest and dividends earned on your investment.

Terms of irrevocable trusts can differ from state to state based on how state Medicaid agencies interpret the rules. Who may serve as trustee may differ. Whether it's possible to name children or others as beneficiaries may vary in different states. For instance, in some states your trust may permit the trustee to make distributions to your children, a so-called "spray" provision, who then may use the distributed funds on your behalf. Other states may track the use of the distributions and determine that you are in fact a beneficiary and therefore all the trust assets must be spent down before you can become eligible for Medicaid. Due to the varied application of the law, it is imperative that these trusts be drafted by attorneys up-to-date on their state's current practices.

TESTAMENTARY TRUSTS

There's an important exception to the rule that if you create a trust for your spouse's benefit and you give the trustee the ability to make distributions of principal to or on behalf of your spouse, the trust funds will be deemed available to be paid for your spouse's care. If, rather than creating and funding the trust during your life, you were to create it in your will, the normal spousal trust rules won't apply. Trusts created in wills are known as "testamentary" trusts (think "last will and testament"). The trustee can have total discretion to make distributions to or on behalf of your surviving spouse without such trust funds being considered available to her in determining her eligibility for Medicaid. Just don't allow your spouse to demand distributions or have the trust require them under any circumstances; they must be discretionary.

Testamentary trusts can be a bit more cumbersome to set up and administer than trusts created during life—so-called *inter vivos* trusts. Your estate will have to be probated to fund them and, depending on the state, the trustees may have to file annual accounts with the probate court. While we discuss the creation of testamentary trusts with all our clients who have spouses receiving Medicaid benefits, many prefer to avoid the hassle of testamentary trusts and leave their estates directly to their children, bypassing their spouses, and relying on their children to care for them and spend money for them as needed. While this is more efficient and cost effective than using a testamentary trust, it carries its own risks. For instance, your children may not agree on how to spend funds on your spouse's behalf, leading to disputes and resentments, especially if some children dip into their pockets for care they deem necessary while others don't.

THIRD-PARTY TRUSTS

Trusts created on your behalf by someone other than yourself or your spouse do not have the same Medicaid deeming rules applied to self-created, or "first party," trusts. Just like testamentary trusts created by a spouse, the funds in a trust created by a third party will only be considered available to you, should you apply for

Medicaid, only if either (a) you have the right to withdraw funds or (b) the trust is required (rather than simply allowed) to disburse funds to you or on your behalf. So, if you are the beneficiary of a trust created by someone other than yourself or your spouse, perhaps a parent or grandparent, you can check the distribution requirements and limitations to determine whether it would be considered available and countable were you or your spouse to apply for Medicaid coverage.

You can also create a third-party trust for your children, grandchildren, or others that would not have to be spent down should they need long-term care but would still be available for them as needed. This is discussed in more depth in the chapters on special needs planning and family protection trusts. If you have no children or grandchildren and may be passing your estate on to your siblings or others in your age cohort, it can be even more important that you leave your estate in trust for their benefit, both so that they don't have to spend down what you leave them to qualify for Medicaid coverage of their care needs, and since most of us become subject to cognitive decline as we age. The older we get, the more important it is to have other qualified people in place to help us manage our finances and investments.

(D)(4)(A) AND (D)(4)(C) TRUSTS

There are two statutory exceptions to the usual rule described above that if you create and fund a trust for your own benefit, its funds will be considered available to you should you apply for Medicaid benefits. Referred to by the federal statute authorizing them, these are commonly referred to as (d)(4)(A) and (d)(4)(C) trusts. The main difference between the two is that (d)(4)(A) trusts are individual trusts that you create for yourself and (d)(4)(C) trusts are managed by non-profit organizations in "pooled" trusts that contain separate accounts for each of any number of beneficiaries.

Both types of trust require that you be disabled when the trust is created and funded, that you be the sole beneficiary of the trust, and that upon your death the state be reimbursed for whatever it has spent on your care through the Medicaid program (for which reason, these trusts are sometimes referred to as "payback" trusts—the varying nomenclature can get confusing). In the unlikely event any funds remain after the state is reimbursed, these can be paid to whomever you name. (There is an important exception to this rule with respect to (d)(4)(C) trusts. The non-profit managing the trust may keep some or all of the trust funds upon the beneficiary's death before any claim by the state Medicaid agency. In some states this right is unlimited, while in others the state permits the non-profit to retain only a set percentage of the remaining funds.)

Given all the above, it would seem that everyone who has a disability would use these trusts. The payback requirement seems like a reasonable tradeoff for getting necessary Medicaid coverage. The problem is the age limitations. (d)(4)(A) trusts must be created and funded before the beneficiary reaches age 65. If this rule has been met, they can still function after the beneficiary is older than 65, but no new funds may be added.

Pooled (d)(4)(C) trusts don't have this requirement. For purposes of Medicaid eligibility, they can be funded at any age. However, there's a gray area on whether the funding of the trusts is subject to the penalty and look-back period for transferring assets. There's an exception to the usual transfer penalty rules for transfers to trusts for the sole benefit of individuals under age 65 who are permanently disabled. This clearly covers transfers to (d)(4)(A) trusts, since they must be created and funded before the beneficiary reaches age 65.

It's less clear whether it covers transfers to (d)(4)(C) trusts. There's a conflict between the transfer rules that have an age limitation and the trust rules that don't. The federal government has left it to the states to interpret this inconsistency as they choose. As a result, some states permit post-age-65 transfers to pooled trusts and some do not.

(D)(4)(B) OR "MILLER" TRUSTS

In reading about (d)(4)(A) and (d)(4)(C) trusts above, you may have wondered, what about (d)(4)(B) trusts? (d)(4)(B) trusts exist as well, but only in some states known as "income cap" states. Just over half the states have no income limits for Medicaid eligibility for nursing home coverage. Nursing home residents simply must pay their income to the facility, less a small personal needs allowance and in some instances a stipend for a healthy spouse. The Medicaid agency then pays the balance of the nursing home fee not covered by the resident's income.

But 24 states (Alabama, Alaska, Arizona, Arkansas, Colorado, Delaware, Florida, Georgia, Idaho, Indiana, Iowa, Kentucky, Louisiana, Mississippi, Nevada, New Mexico, New Jersey, Oklahoma, Oregon, South Carolina, South Dakota, Tennessee, Texas, and Wyoming) are so-called "income cap" states. They have an absolute monthly income limit of $2,382 (in 2021) for eligibility for Medicaid coverage. If your income exceeds this cap by even $1, you can't qualify for Medicaid. Or, at least, you can't without sheltering the excess income in a trust. Often known as "Miller" trusts, referring to the Colorado court case that initially authorized their use, these trusts permit nursing home residents to pay their excess income over the income cap to a qualifying trust and then for the trust to pay it over to the nursing home. This workaround was codified in the same statute that brought us (d)(4)(A) and (d)(4)(C) trusts, with the rules set out in subsection (d)(4)(B) of the same statute. You may wonder why this extra step for Medicaid eligibility is necessary. So do I.

CHAPTER 13
SPECIAL NEEDS TRUSTS

Special needs trusts are used to hold assets for individuals with disabilities for two purposes: so the funds will be well managed and so the beneficiary may qualify for public benefits, such as Medicaid, Supplemental Security Income (SSI), and subsidized housing. They are usually created either by parents or grandparents for children and grandchildren who have special needs or by an individual with savings who, due to injury or illness, becomes disabled as an adult. In the latter case, funds often come as the result of the settlement of personal injury lawsuits for the accident that caused the disability.

You may come across the term "supplemental needs" trust, which refers to the concept that the beneficiary's basic needs will be supplied by available public benefits programs, with the trust reserved to supplement what they provide. This term, however, has fallen by the wayside in recent years. You may also notice that some of what follows mirrors the discussion in Chapter 12 on Medicaid Planning. This is because Medicaid planning is generally done for people who become disabled in later life and involves similar public benefit and trust concepts.

TRUSTS FOR CHILDREN AND GRANDCHILDREN

While all parents must plan to make sure that their minor children will be taken care of in the event of the parents' death or disability, for parents of children with special needs, these concerns never end. Depending on the level of disability, these children will depend on their parents for financial and emotional support and guidance for the parents' lifetimes and beyond.

More families are dealing with these issues than ever before, due to advances in medical care: more people with congenital disabilities or injuries are living longer; premature babies are surviving with ailments; victims of accidents of all sorts are surviving. At the same time, as health care becomes more complex and more high-tech, it has also become more expensive (not to mention that health care in the United States costs more than twice what it costs in every other developed nation). The maintenance of eligibility for Medicaid to cover health care costs can be vital, as is coverage by other public programs.

Financial planning, therefore, needs to cover not only the parents' retirement and long-term care needs, but ongoing support for any children with special needs. (Presumably, other children will be able to fend for themselves.) The challenges include:

- Making sure the funds you leave your child with a disability benefit her without causing her to lose important public benefits,

- Making sure funds are well managed,

- Assuring that your other children are not overburdened with caring for their disabled sibling, and that any burdens fall relatively evenly among the siblings,

- Trying to be fair in terms of distributing your estate between your disabled child and your other children, and

- Making sure there's enough money to meet your disabled child's needs, as well as figuring out what is enough.

Parents of children with special needs may try to resolve these issues by leaving their estates to their other children, and nothing to the disabled children. At first glance this appears to solve several challenges: The disabled child shouldn't receive anything because she can't manage money and would lose her benefits. She doesn't need any inheritance because she will be taken care of by the public benefits she receives. The other children will take care of their sibling.

This approach is discouraged for a number of reasons: First, public benefits programs are usually inadequate. They need to be supplemented with other resources. Second, both public benefits programs and individual circumstances change over time. What's working today may not work tomorrow. Other resources need to be available, just in case. Third, relying on one's other children to take care of their sibling could place an undue burden on them and strain relations between them. It makes it unclear whether inherited money belongs to the healthy child to spend as he pleases, or whether he must set it aside for his disabled sibling. If one child sets money aside, and the others don't, resentments can build that may split the family forever.

In essence, a special needs trust is a discretionary trust, permitting the trustee to use the trust funds as it deems appropriate for the beneficiary. The beneficiary has no right to demand payment of trust funds or to depend on it for support. It's this wording that assures that the trust funds will not be counted in determining the beneficiary's eligibility for public benefits, or for that matter, being subject to claims by creditors of the beneficiary, or an ex-spouse in the event of a divorce. Depending on the source of the funds and whether the parents have particular tax or other planning goals, the exact terms of the trust will be tailored to meet those objectives.

All of this discussion assumes that the money, investments, or real estate funding the trust are coming from the parents or grandparents. These are sometimes called "third-party" trusts because the donor and the beneficiary are not the same person. The rules of public benefits programs regarding trusts are much more strict if the applicant for coverage has a trust funded with his own money, sometimes referred to as "first-party" trusts.

Special needs trusts may be revocable or irrevocable. Often they are revocable if they will be funded only by the parents, but irrevocable if grandparents or others may also contribute to them. Otherwise, if the grandparents contribute to a revocable trust created by the parents, for all practical purposes such funds will belong to the parents during their lives. Some lawyers always make special needs trusts irrevocable just in case others may contribute, reasoning that until they're funded they are effectively revocable, since the parents can always tear them up and start over.

PERSONAL INJURY SETTLEMENTS

People with disabilities can receive substantial funds, whether due to settling a personal injury lawsuit or receiving an inheritance. And some people become disabled later in life as the result of a personal injury after they have accumulated savings. In most cases, these individuals do not have enough funds to support themselves indefinitely and must depend on public benefits, such as SSI, subsidized housing, Medicaid, and SNAP, for their basic support. Frequently, getting money disrupts a carefully constructed system of support that depends on eligibility for various public benefits programs. Either way, preserving eligibility for benefits can be vital for the individual with a disability. In addition, if the disability is cognitive in nature, the beneficiary may not be able to handle the funds or may be vulnerable to financial abuse by others.

As with parents planning for their children, trusts can provide a solution. However, the trusts must be different. For the property and income in these so-called "self-settled" trusts not to be taken into account in determining the beneficiary's eligibility for benefits, they must meet specific requirements set out in federal law at 42 USC § 1396p(d)(4)(A) and (d)(4)(C). As a result, these are often referred to as "(d)(4)(A)" and "(d)(4)(C)" trusts. The main difference between the two is that (d)(4)(A) trusts are individual trusts for each beneficiary and (d)(4)(C) trusts are managed for many beneficiaries by non-profit organizations. But there are also some specific differences, described below.

Often personal injury claimants are advised to "structure" their settlements. A structure is an annuity, providing set annual or monthly payments over time rather than providing the full settlement as a lump sum. Structures provide certain tax advantages and can help ensure that funds continue to flow in, so they're not lost to poor spending and financial decisions or to financial predators. However, the income stream from a structure can make the recipient ineligible for public benefits. So, even if some or all of a settlement is to be structured, it can be important that the payments are made to a special needs trust.

(D)(4)(A) TRUSTS

Medicaid would count the funds in most trusts you created for yourself or for your spouse as being available if either of you were to apply for benefits. However, the Medicaid rules under 42 USC § 1396b(d)(4)(A) and (C) provide for two "safe harbor" trusts that are exceptions to the general trust rules. The first, referred to as a (d)(4)(A) trust (or "payback" trust, referring to one of its key features, explained below) may be created by the applicant for Medicaid benefits or by her parent, grandparent, guardian, or a court, for the sole benefit of a disabled individual under age 65. It may be funded with the disabled individual's own funds, and the trust property will not be considered available in determining the disabled individual's eligibility for Medicaid benefits as long as the trust provides that at the beneficiary's death, the state will be reimbursed out of any remaining trust funds for Medicaid benefits paid on behalf of the beneficiary during his or her life.

Transfers into a (d)(4)(A) or (d)(4)(C) trust (described below) are not penalized, whether the trust is for the Medicaid applicant's benefit or that of another individual who is disabled and under age 65 at the time of the transfer. While (with some exceptions) the beneficiary has to be under age 65 when creating and funding these trusts, they continue to serve their role of sheltering assets for purposes of Medicaid and SSI eligibility even after the beneficiary passes age 65.

These trusts are incredibly valuable planning devices for people under age 65 who are disabled, whether the disability arose at birth or at a later age. The tradeoff of having to reimburse Medicaid with funds remaining at death in exchange for getting benefits, both Medicaid and SSI, during life, is almost always worth it. But there can be exceptions, such as in the following case that occurred in our office.

We prepared a (d)(4)(A) trust for a man in his early 50s who had been injured in a motorcycle accident. The trust sheltered his personal injury settlement that resulted from the accident. It came several years after the accident, during which time he incurred large medical costs covered by Medicaid. Unfortunately, his family contacted us just a year or two later when the man died. Almost all the trust money went to reimburse the state for the man's medical expenses it had paid out prior to settlement of his lawsuit. This would not have been the case had we not set up the trust because Medicaid's normal claim for reimbursement is only for benefits paid after age 55 or for payments for nursing home care at any age. Of course, when we set up the trust, we did not expect our client's imminent death and this predated the Affordable Care Act, so private insurance was not available due to his preexisting conditions. In addition, Medicaid paid for the man's personal care attendants, which are not covered by private insurance in any case. So, it was probably the right decision to use a (d)(4)(A) trust, but with unfortunate consequences for the family.

While the beneficiary must be under age 65 when the trust is funded, the trust retains its exempt status for the rest of her life. You may well ask why everyone doesn't put some money into a (d)(4)(A) trust before age 65 just in case they need Medicaid in the future. The payback provision is not a problem if you don't use Medicaid, so that's not a drawback. The problem is that the trust does not qualify unless you are disabled when you fund it.

To review, in order for a (d)(4)(A) trust to qualify, it must meet the following requirements:

- It must be irrevocable.

- The beneficiary must be under age 65 and disabled at the time of funding. Anyone who is receiving Social Security Disability Insurance (SSDI) or SSI is automatically deemed to be disabled. Beneficiaries who are not receiving these benefits will have to go through a certification process as determined by each state.

- The trust must be created by the beneficiary, a court, or the beneficiary's parent, grandparent, or guardian.

- The disabled individual must be the only beneficiary during his life.

- At the beneficiary's death, all state Medicaid programs that have paid for his care during his life must be reimbursed for their costs. If funds remain after such reimbursements, they can be distributed to the beneficiary's estate or to others named in the trust.

(D)(4)(C) TRUSTS

Similar to (d)(4)(A) or payback trusts, (d)(4)(C), or "pooled disability" trusts, permit disabled individuals to shelter assets and still qualify for Medicaid and SSI. Where a (d)(4)(A) trust is an individual trust managed by a trustee chosen by the grantor, a (d)(4)(C) trust is a pooled trust managed by a non-profit organization. Other differences and similarities are as follows:

- For both, the beneficiary must be disabled as defined by the Social Security Administration. In general, if you qualify for SSI or SSDI, you meet the disability requirement. If you haven't applied for either program, you will have to meet the screening requirements of your state.

- The disabled individual, her parent, grandparent, guardian, or a court must fund the trust. For either trust, it should be funded with the beneficiary's own assets, not those contributed by someone else.

- Both types of trusts have a requirement that at the beneficiary's death the state be repaid for Medicaid expenditures made on her behalf, but there's a carve out for (d)(4)(C) trusts. They can hold money back for their own purposes. While the federal law permits them to withhold all of the remaining trust funds and pay no estate recovery, some states have limited the amount of the hold back.

- While a (d)(4)(A) trust must be funded before the beneficiary reaches age 65, a (d)(4)(C) trust has no such restriction. However, the states are inconsistent on whether they penalize transfers to (d)(4)(C) trusts after age 65, some penalizing such transfers and some not doing so. To clarify this point, if you are 70 years old and disabled, and you transfer $50,000 into a (d)(4)(C) trust, the funds in that trust will not be counted in any state in determining your eligibility for SSI or Medicaid. However, in some states if you apply for Medicaid benefits during the five-year lookback period that follows the transfer, you will be ineligible for coverage for a period of time based on the amount transferred. In other states, you will not be penalized. In the latter states, this option can be very useful for nursing home residents who can transfer funds to a (d)(4)(C) trust, qualify for Medicaid benefits to cover the basic nursing home cost, but still have some money on the side to pay for extras, whether that's special aides, travel outside the facility, additional therapy, or anything else the senior may need or want. This is not, however, a way to save money to leave family members, since any funds remaining upon the senior's death will either remain in the trust or reimburse the state for its Medicaid expenditures on the beneficiary's behalf.

So, when would you want to use a (d)(4)(C) trust as opposed to a (d)(4)(A) trust? They both protect assets and provide for eligibility for Medicaid and SSI. Certainly, if you are over 65 and are in a state where the transfer into the trust is not penalized, you would use a (d)(4)(C) trust. For others, here are some factors to consider:

- **The amount of money to put in the trust.** Larger amounts justify the cost of creating a separate trust and perhaps of paying a professional trustee. For smaller amounts, it's usually more cost-effective to use the already existing structure of a (d)(4)(C) trust.

- **The availability of an appropriate trustee.** You may have a trusted and reliable family member or friend who is willing and able to serve as trustee. If you don't have anyone you can rely on to maintain the trust, following the rules both for administering trusts and for maintaining eligibility for public benefits, the (d)(4)(C) trust may be your best alternative.

- **Control.** You will have more of a sense of control if someone you're close to is the trustee or a co-trustee of your trust. With a (d)(4)(C) trust, decisions will be made according to the trust's rules and policies, disbursement requests sometimes being responded to by committee.

To learn about the (d)(4)(C) trusts available in your community, the Academy of Special Needs Planners maintains a nationwide list of pooled disability trusts at www.specialneedsanswers.com/pooled-trust.

CHOICE OF TRUSTEE

Often, choosing a trustee is the most difficult part of planning for a child with special needs. Since the individual with special needs will likely need the trust to last for her lifetime and will have no claim to the funds except as decided upon by the trustees, the selection of trustees is especially important. And of course, no one can truly replace parents in looking after their child with special needs.

The trustee of a supplemental needs trust must be able to fulfill all the normal functions of a trustee—accounting, investments, tax returns and distributions—and also meet the needs of the special beneficiary. The latter can include an understanding of various public benefits programs, sensitivity to the beneficiary's particular style of communication, and knowledge of services that may be available. Often family members have the necessary emotional attachment but don't have the experience, expertise, or available time to handle the financial and legal aspects of serving as trustee. Professionals, such as lawyers and bank trustees, have the financial and legal experience necessary, but may not know the beneficiary well or be equipped to respond to the needs of a beneficiary who may be more demanding than their typical client. However, they may be able to hire a care manager who has the skills and knowledge to fill in the trustee's own gaps.

Qualities of good trustees for any trust—and especially for a special needs trust—include:

- the ability to make sound financial decisions, invest prudently, and properly report trust transactions;

- an understanding of the rules around eligibility for public benefits, or a willingness to learn;
- availability and the time to spend to perform the duties needed;
- honesty and integrity; and
- emotional attachment to the beneficiary.

There are a number of possible solutions available for finding a trustee or trustees who satisfy these requirements. Often parents choose to appoint co-trustees—a bank or law firm as a professional trustee along with another child or an aunt or uncle as a family trustee. Working together, they can provide the necessary resources and experience to meet the needs of the child with special needs. Unfortunately, in many cases such a combination is not available. Professional trustees generally require a minimum amount of funds in the trust, usually at least $500,000. Otherwise their fees become unreasonable in relation to the size of the trust. In other situations, there is no appropriate family member to appoint as co-trustee.

When no appropriate family member is available to serve as co-trustee, the parent may direct the professional trustee to consult with named individuals who know and care for the child with special needs. These could be family members who are not appropriate trustees, but who can serve in an advisory role. Or they may be social workers or others who have both personal and professional knowledge of the beneficiary and the resources available for her care. This role may be formalized in the trust document as a "care committee."

Often special needs trusts appoint one or more "trust protectors" who have the power to hire and fire trustees, appoint a successor trustee if the current trustee resigns or becomes incapacitated, review trust accounts and make limited amendments to the trust. This can be a good role for family members or friends whom you trust, but who live too far away, don't have the time available, or are otherwise inappropriate to serve as trustee.

TRUST FUNDING

A number of issues arise with respect to the question of how much to put into the trust. First, how much will the child with special needs require over her life? Second, should parents leave the same portion of their estate to all of their children, no matter their need? Third, how will they assure that there's enough money to meet everyone's needs?

The first question is a difficult one. It depends on what assumptions are made about the child's needs and the availability of other resources to fulfill those needs. Financial planners who work in this field can help make projections to assist with this determination. But in all cases, it's better to err on the side of more money rather than less. You can't be certain current programs will continue. And you have to factor in paying for services, such as case management, that the parents provide free of charge every day.

If these assumptions mean that the child with special needs will require a large percentage of his parents' estate, how will his siblings feel if they receive less than their pro rata share? After all, the estate may already be smaller than it would be otherwise due to the time and money spent providing for the child with special needs. And the other children may feel they have received less parental attention growing up than they would have otherwise, had they not had a sibling with special needs. On the other hand, brothers and sisters may understand that life is not always "fair," realize that their sibling with special needs is unable to provide financially, as they are, and be grateful that the parents are able to continue providing through a trust so the burden does not fall on the younger generation. Many scenarios are possible.

One solution to the question of fairness and to the challenge of assuring that there are enough funds is life insurance. Parents can divide their estate equally among their children, but supplement the amount going to the special needs trust with life insurance. Unlike life insurance purchased to take care of minor children, which may be term insurance, insurance to fund a special needs trust should be permanent—whole or universal. Unfortunately, such policies are much more expensive than term insurance. This can sometimes be an area where grandparents can help. The parents may be financially strapped and unable to pay for the insurance, but their parents may be able do so on their behalf. Also, be aware that it often makes sense to lower the premiums through a second-to-die policy, paying out only when the second parent passes away, which is when the money will probably be needed to cover additional care.

CHAPTER 14
ASSET PROTECTION TRUSTS

Trusts can be used to protect assets from creditors in the event of bankruptcy, lawsuit or divorce. But the rules of such asset protection trusts are very different, depending on whether you or a third party creates and funds the trust for your benefit. The rule under traditional, or "common law," trust law is that if you create a trust for your own benefit, to the extent the property in the trust is available to you, it's also available to your creditors. You can, however, create a trust for someone else—often called a "third-party" trust—and write it in such a way that it will be protected from her creditors. The upcoming chapter on family protection trusts discusses how you might create such trusts for the benefit of your children and grandchildren. Here, however, are three ways around this rule precluding asset protection for self-settled trusts for your own benefit.

IRREVOCABLE TRUSTS

The first is to create an irrevocable trust that restricts your access. For instance, you can create a trust that pays out the interest, dividends, or rental income to you, but which completely restricts your access to principal. In essence, you're giving up your access to trust property in exchange for protection of that property. These trusts are often used in the context of planning for Medicaid coverage of nursing home care, as explained in Chapter 12. You might also title real estate in such a trust, preserving only the right to use and occupy the property. In any of these trusts, beware of the tax consequences and the differing state rules on "Medicaid-qualifying" trusts.

THIRD-PARTY TRUSTS

The second option is to create a trust for the benefit of a third party, such as a spouse or child who you want to provide for or who could share the trust benefit with you if necessary, though legally they would not be required to do so. This is a third-party trust: one you create for someone other than yourself, but which carries out a goal or goals towards which you might normally spend funds. This may be easier with a spouse, since if the trust, for instance, pays all housing costs for your spouse and you happen to live in the house as well, you will still reap a benefit. If, on the other hand, a child funnels trust distributions back to you, the trust may be treated as a sham since you may be deemed as the true beneficiary. So, if you're transferring your own funds into a trust for asset protection purposes, be sure that you're ready to give up access to such property.

Hybrids of the first two approaches may also be available. For instance, you may create a trust that permits distributions of income to you and principal to your children and grandchildren.

To expand on the concept of creating an asset protection trust for your spouse, you can do so while you are still alive or after your death. Trusts used for estate tax protection as described in Chapter 11 can serve this purpose, as long as the surviving spouse does not serve as trustee and has no right to withdraw principal. If you create an asset protection trust for your spouse during your life, as with a trust for your children, make sure the funds are not funneled back to you. And don't create reciprocal trusts. If you and your spouse create and fund identical trusts for one another, they lose their protection because you're not really giving away your assets. Instead you're doing so in exchange for a benefit—your spouse's trust.

DOMESTIC ASSET PROTECTION TRUSTS (DAPTS)

The third option is to take advantage of the laws in those states that have overturned the "common law" and permitted the creation of self-settled asset protection trusts, so-called domestic asset protection trusts or DAPTs (as opposed to offshore trusts, long an asset-protection strategy of the very wealthy). Led by Alaska, Delaware, Nevada, and South Dakota, thirteen additional states (Hawaii, Michigan, Mississippi, Missouri, New Hampshire, Ohio, Oklahoma, Rhode Island, Tennessee, Utah, Virginia, West Virginia, and Wyoming) currently permit such trusts. Each state has its own rules, but typically they require that the trust property be held in a financial institution within its state and that at least one trustee— whether institutional or individual—be from that state. While you cannot serve as trustee, you can appoint someone you trust—perhaps your lawyer or accountant or a close family member—to serve as "trust protector" with certain rights, such as the ability to change trustees, to amend the trust as needed to comply with changes in the law, or even to change beneficiaries.

So far, there have been few cases actually testing these DAPTs and statutes. Their proponents argue that even where the trusts might be challenged, such challenges would be litigated and at the very least the cost and uncertainty of such litigation would serve as a hurdle to recovery, thus making a favorable settlement of a claim much more likely. In addition, the states that have passed DAPT statutes have an interest in upholding them, since they bring significant business to their banks.

At best, the trusts totally protect the assets they hold from creditors. Since these trusts are somewhat expensive to set up and administer (and potentially to defend in court), they are generally used by people of high net worth in potentially risky businesses—such as medical professionals who may be sued for malpractice. If you would be interested in pursuing an out-of-state asset protection trust, you will need to consult with a specialist in the field. Be aware that the fraudulent conveyance rules apply to these trusts, meaning that you cannot use them to protect assets from claims that already exist, just from potential future claims.

OFFSHORE TRUSTS

A fourth option, but one which few readers of this book will consider using, is offshore trusts. A number of island nations have created laws protecting funds in trusts created and administered from their shores. The DAPT industry in some ways grew up as a reaction to the offshore option in an effort to keep the funds and business in the United States. It isn't clear what the benefit of going offshore would be, now that DAPTs are available, unless the purpose is to hide funds and income from the U.S. authorities, either because they are illicit or to avoid taxation, neither of which we would condone.

CHAPTER 15
FAMILY PROTECTION TRUSTS

In Chapter 14 on asset protection trusts, we focused on how you can use a trust to protect your own assets from loss in a lawsuit, bankruptcy proceeding or divorce, along with the restrictions on such trusts. As mentioned in that chapter, it is much easier to use trusts to protect assets you give to someone else, presumably your child or grandchild. The law permits you to place limitations on the beneficiary's access to the funds that also protects them from creditors, in the event of divorce, and from being taxed upon the beneficiary's death.

As is discussed below, these trusts are often called "spendthrift" or "generation-skipping" trusts. The latter term refers to the fact that the trust funds are not taxed in the estate of the first generation of beneficiaries. This is less of an issue today with very few estates subject to federal estate tax at all. In our practice, we call such trusts "family protection" trusts.

SPENDTHRIFT TRUSTS

The common law has always permitted donors to create trusts for others that would not be subject to the beneficiary's creditors. These are often called "spendthrift" trusts because they are designed to protect beneficiaries from their own bad decisions, as well as to keep funds in the family. To work, the trust must not require any distributions to the beneficiary or beneficiaries nor give them any right to demand distributions. Instead, it can be discretionary, meaning that the trustee has full authority to determine when, whether, and how to make distributions to beneficiaries directly or on their behalf, and it must contain language barring beneficiaries from pledging or conveying their interests in the trust. While the trust might give the trustee complete discretion, it can also be limited, for instance permitting only distribution of income, or only distributions that permit the beneficiary to maintain his current standard of living.

With these provisions, such trusts are protected from the beneficiaries' creditors. But the result is that they can be very restrictive. This apocryphal story shows how restrictive they can be:

> A young Harvard student goes into the Boston business district to meet with the gray-haired trustee of his trust to ask for money to buy a new suit. This, of course, was back in the days when Harvard students wore suits. The trustee responds: "When I was at Harvard, I had one suit that lasted me all four years." Before continuing, he pauses to pick some lint off of his sleeve. "In fact, it's still standing up pretty well today."

Not surprisingly, the Harvard student's request for funds to buy a new suit was denied. One moral of the story is that, when planning your estate and the protections you want to provide your heirs, the more protective a trust is, the more restrictive it is as well. A second moral of the story is to pick your trustee well and provide her guidance, whether in the trust document itself or in a side memorandum, so she carries out your intent rather than simply imposing her own judgment and values. The trustee in this case may or may not have been carrying out the wishes of the person who created the trust. In other words, he may have been applying his own frugal values rather than those of the trust creator.

FAMILY PROTECTION TRUSTS

In our practice, we often prepare for our clients what we call "family protection" trusts (borrowing the name from my colleague Michael Gilfix of Gilfix & La Poll Associates in Palo Alto, California) in order to protect what they pass on to their children and grandchildren. Assets in such trusts are protected from creditors, in the event of divorce, and if their child dies early. In the latter case, the inheritance continues in trust for the grandchildren rather than passing to the surviving spouse and potentially ultimately out of the family. With respect to the last goal, the trust may give the child a power of appointment to have the funds go to the surviving spouse if that's what the child would prefer.

In an attempt to balance protection with practicality, we typically design the trusts as follows:

1. We create a separate trust for each beneficiary.

2. The beneficiary (usually a child) may serve as trustee and even as the only trustee.

3. But while she may manage and invest the trust funds as she sees fit, she may distribute only income (and not principal) to herself.

4. If she needs access to principal, she must appoint an independent trustee who would have discretion to either distribute principal for her benefit or refuse to do so.

This trust design is meant to provide protection while responding to the reluctance of many clients (and their children) to give up control. It will work as long as the child actually follows the rules of the trust; its Achilles heel is that the beneficiary has access to the trust property and could easily drain the trust. This would violate the terms of the trust and make any remaining funds vulnerable to lawsuit, divorce or bankruptcy. It would also make the trustee liable to a claim by the remainder beneficiaries, but since they would likely be his children or siblings. they would probably be unlikely to sue him. In addition, if he's the type of person who would drain the trust, he also may be likely to spend the trust assets and not have other assets available to pay the resulting judgment won by his children. Even if the beneficiary trustee does not completely drain the trust but starts spending some of the principal, he will undermine its protection, making it more vulnerable in lawsuits by creditors or a spouse. This means that the trustee needs careful instruction when the family protection trust is funded.

Appointing an independent trustee from the outset is definitely more secure. But most clients are put off by the expense of the trustee fees and the lack of control of putting someone else in charge. Often this is a penny wise, pound foolish attitude because professional trustees can quickly earn their fees through their investment and management expertise, as well as making sure the trust fulfills its purpose. Unfortunately, many clients sacrifice safety in the interest of avoiding payment of professional trustee fees.

So, in determining whether to create a family protection trust and whether to name a family member or an independent trustee, you will need to balance your children's and grandchildren's need for protection and their likely level of responsibility. While bad things, financial and otherwise, can happen to anyone, those most likely to need protection may also be more likely to need an independent trustee.

TAX PROTECTIONS

In addition to creditor and divorce protection, family protection trusts also offer tax protection since the funds in the trust will not be included in the child's taxable estate. For this reason, they are sometimes referred to as "generation-skipping" trusts, since the ultimate distribution goes to the grandchildren, skipping the children (though they are usually beneficiaries during their lives). Because a lot of rich families were using these trusts to avoid taxation at the passing of each generation, allowing accumulated wealth to continue potentially for centuries, Congress enacted a "generation-skipping" tax. This gets very complicated, but the bottom line is that it limits how much can pass tax free from generation to generation. With the current very high threshold for federal estate taxation, which is shared by the generation-skipping tax, very few taxpayers have to be concerned about either. If you do have a federally taxable estate, you need to work with a qualified estate planning attorney. One source of such qualified attorneys for larger estates is the American College of Trust and Estate Counsel (ACTEC) at www.actec.org.

KEEPING IT IN THE FAMILY

For the less wealthy, family protection trusts also keep assets in the family in the event of the premature death of a child. If an adult child directly inherits funds and then passes away, those funds will likely pass to the deceased child's spouse. The spouse may remarry, have additional children, and even become estranged from the children of his first marriage (we have seen this happen). Those children may then receive none of the property that came from their grandparents. If, instead, the grandparents had left the funds in a family protection trust, at the death of the parent they would remain in trust for the benefit of her children.

CHAPTER 16
SECOND-MARRIAGE TRUSTS

When you marry for the first time, it is likely you are young(ish), have no children, and have little by way of assets. Life is relatively simple. If you're marrying or are in a committed relationship for the second, third, or fourth time, your personal and financial lives are likely to be a bit more complicated. You may have children from one or more prior relationships, as may your partner. You may be bringing substantial assets to the relationship; and if you're a widow or widower, you may have accumulated those through a lifetime of work, saving, and planning with your prior spouse. Your children may have an expectation regarding such assets.

All too often, we see clients and others fall into these new relationships without much thought or discussion about financial issues. This can lead to unintended results—often with the assets of both spouses ending up in the name of the surviving spouse and whatever remains after she has died going to her family or being spent down completely on her long-term care. Whether or not this outcome is what the deceased spouse or partner wanted, it can lead to significant resentment if this is not communicated to his family.

A few basic steps can lead to much better outcomes and understanding.

TALK IT OVER

If you're getting married or you're in a committed relationship and this is not your first gig, start by having a full discussion of your expectations—both during life and after death. Who is going to pay for what? What financial support should either of you expect after the other passes away? What will happen when and if one of you needs care? Simply making assumptions or letting come what comes can lead to conflict and undesirable results. In almost all circumstances, one of you will die before the other. If you leave everything to your children, it could leave your partner high and dry, perhaps having to move at the same time she is grieving your loss. If you leave everything to your partner, even if she intends to share equally with your children at her death, this may not occur if she spends everything down paying for long-term care, loses contact with your children over time, or develops a stronger allegiance to her own children and grandchildren or to a new partner. She may change her plan. Or, if she does fall ill or become demented, her own children may step in to take care of her and take steps to protect her assets from the costs of long-term care, favoring themselves in the process.

The discussion can be difficult, in no small part because relationships don't deepen all at once; they develop over time. But two changes in circumstances should definitely lead to the discussion: moving in together and getting married. And the discussion should happen for both events, since presumably your commitment to each other will be somewhat different when you take these steps. And marriage, of course, is a legal relationship, as well as a personal and romantic one.

PUT IT IN WRITING

Once you've clarified your expectations, they need to be implemented through a written agreement. This can be as formal as a prenuptial agreement or as informal as a handwritten document. Putting your expectations in writing serves several important purposes, including:

- Making sure you're both on the same page about your expectations.

- Raising issues you hadn't thought about. The act of putting pen to paper raises new questions that may not have been obvious otherwise.

- Aiding memory. None of us remembers everything perfectly, and our memories can change over time. Having a written agreement about what you agreed to years ago can help refresh and correct your memory.

- Informing others who might get involved. Your children probably have their own expectations about how things will work out and what your intentions might be. To avoid arguments about what your wishes might have been, you need to put them in writing.

Remember, as your relationship changes over time, you can always change the "deal." As long as both partners agree, you can change whatever agreement you made at the outset.

UPDATE YOUR ESTATE PLAN

Whatever you have in place before you get into your new relationship probably is not what you want afterwards. Who do you want to serve as your health care agent? As your agent under your durable power of attorney? Who should receive your life insurance or retirement benefits? Do you want your new partner to be able to remain in your house if you pass away first? For how long?

This is where a second-marriage (or relationship) trust can come in. You might want your home or some of your assets to remain in trust for your spouse or partner, to then go to your children after he dies. This raises a number of issues that need to be discussed. Who should serve as trustee? There's always the risk that the surviving spouse will drain the trust. What happens if he moves out of the house?

One piece of advice: If possible, don't make your children wait until your spouse or partner dies before they get anything from your estate, especially if you're both relatively young or your spouse is significantly younger than you. That could be a long wait. You don't want your children hanging around like vultures waiting for your spouse to die, or for them to be subject to his whim in terms of whether there's anything left for them. It's far better that they receive something upon your death. If necessary, buy life insurance to make sure this happens.

LET EVERYONE (WHO SHOULD KNOW) KNOW

Finally, let your families know about your plan. The more transparency you have with your partner and your children, the better. Even if you do everything else right, a lack of communication can have drastic pitfalls—as this case handled in our office will illustrate.

Our clients, whom we'll call Paul and Georgina, were a committed couple in their early 60s who were not married but planned to live together for the rest of their lives. They each had two children from prior marriages. They were both still working full time. They executed trusts through which they would leave their own property in trust for the survivor of the two with whatever was left in trust when the survivor died to be split equally among the four children. They were each co-trustees of each other's trust.

Tragically, soon thereafter Paul died from a massive heart attack. Unfortunately, his children thought he was much wealthier than he was and that Georgina was holding out on them. Under their father's trust, they had the right to change trustees. We included that in the document to protect them in case the surviving partner began mismanaging the trust. In retrospect, this was a mistake. They removed Georgina and named an independent attorney as trustee. This worked terribly. This new trustee made no effort to contact Georgina and failed to take necessary steps to protect a retirement plan from adverse tax consequences. He also didn't make the required distributions of income from the trust to Georgina.

Once Paul's children were convinced that the money they thought Paul had didn't exist, they and their attorney simply stopped responding. Ultimately, we had to bring a lawsuit to remove the new trustee. While the new trustee had to pay some damages as a result of his mismanagement, those damages did not approach Georgina's out-of-pocket costs nor compensate her for the stress she went through. Not surprisingly, she eventually changed her own estate plan so that her assets will ultimately go only to her children.

If Paul's children had had a better understanding of his estate and his plans, they might have been more likely to have accepted it. Could the plan have been different? Perhaps. Paul could have given his children something immediately to keep them happy, rather than having to wait for Georgina's death to get anything. Was it a mistake to give Paul's children the power to change trustees? In retrospect, yes. But what if Georgina failed to send them annual accounts over the years, or began to raid the trust, or became demented? Simply changing trustees could prevent an expensive and stressful action in court. In short, this plan did not achieve all the results Paul and Georgina were seeking, but it did achieve a lot of them. After the litigation ended and Georgina paid off Paul's children with a small settlement, she had the financial security that Paul had intended. With no plan in place, his assets would have gone to his children, who clearly would not have had Georgina's interests at heart.

CHAPTER 17
TRUSTS FOR MINOR CHILDREN

Most estate plans that provide for minor children or children in their early 20s provide that any funds left to them be held and managed for their benefit until they reach a certain age—often 25. Boilerplate provisions in wills and trusts often contain the same rules for any beneficiary who is under the specified age. Typically these trusts simply give the executor or trustee the right to hold the funds in trust for the underage beneficiary as it deems best, to use them for her benefit, or to transfer them to someone else, such as a guardian, to use for her benefit. Any funds remaining when the beneficiary "comes of age" are then to be distributed to her.

But there are a number of options that can make the trusts more useful. The following are choices an estate planning attorney is likely to ask the client to consider when drafting a trust for minor children.

"POT" TRUST VS. SHARES

One question is whether the trust should stay as a single fund for all the children in the family—which estate planners often call a "pot" trust—or be divided into separate shares for each child.

It's certainly easier for a trustee to manage a single fund rather than several separate shares. But this may result in an unequal distribution of the total funds. For example, if there is a pot trust and more money is spent on one child's education, it creates a smaller pool to be divided when the beneficiaries all come of age. But should a child in effect be "charged" for his greater need (college education) by reducing his own inheritance when he becomes older? You could make an argument either way, though many parents figure that their children should not be charged for money spent on basic education. But perhaps for money extended to purchase a home, to pursue graduate school, or to engage in other "optional" activities, it is more "fair" to have the funds come from an individual share.

One option is to hold the funds together until the youngest child reaches age 18 and then divide it into shares. Or perhaps until age 22 if you don't feel that the varied costs of college tuition should be charged to individual children. Of course, this plan may mean that the older children have to wait until after age 25 to get their shares. The bigger the range in age among the children, the more sense it makes to divide the fund into shares at an earlier age.

AGE OF DISTRIBUTION

Earlier, I mentioned age 25 as a typical age when trusts for younger children end, but this may make more sense in some cases than in others. Parents and grandparents need to consider the size of the funds and the maturity of their offspring, both of which may be hard to know if both parents and children are young. Certainly, getting to age 25 means that most beneficiaries will have finished all or the bulk of their schooling. For purposes of financial aid, it's better that funds be in trust rather than held by the student himself. By age 25, the beneficiary will likely be more mature and better able to handle the money than at age 22.

But he may be even more mature and experienced at age 30 or 35. As a result, trusts holding larger amounts of funds often divide the distributions over time, with the beneficiary perhaps receiving half at age 25 and half at age 30, or a third at such ages with the final third being distributed at age 35. Not only will the beneficiary be more likely to be more mature at these ages, but the experience of managing the early distribution or distributions may help him better manage the later ones.

Of course, there are also the benefits, discussed in Chapter 15 about family protection trusts, of never requiring full distribution of the trust funds.

PURPOSE

Often trusts for minor children are rather vague about how trusts are to be used for their benefit, leaving this to the trustees' discretion. But you have the option of being specific: saying, for instance, that the trust should pay for summer camp; for travel, whether recreational, educational, or to visit family members; and for education. For older children, you might provide for distribution upon marriage or to pay the down payment for a home. Options abound and are discussed in more detail in Chapter 20 on purpose trusts.

DEATH OF CHILD

While it's unlikely with younger beneficiaries, it's possible that one will die before complete distribution of his share. Just in case, the trust must provide what will happen with the remaining funds. In most cases, trusts provide that they will pass to that child's children, if any, and, if none, to his siblings. The trust may also give each beneficiary the right to say where his share will go through the exercise of a testamentary power of appointment. This power may be broad, permitting distribution to anyone, or more narrow—perhaps just to family members, a spouse, and charities. Younger beneficiaries are unlikely to take advantage of the power of appointment, but if the trust might continue until they reach age 30 or 35, they're more likely to do so.

CHAPTER 18
TRUSTS FOR RETIREMENT PLANS

There are a lot of reasons you may want some or all of your retirement plan assets to go into trust for the benefit of your heirs, including:

- Estate tax planning.

- In a second (or subsequent) relationship, to provide for your current partner or spouse but to make sure remaining funds go to your children.

- To protect inherited IRAs from creditors (the Supreme Court has ruled that credit protection for inherited IRAs is not as strong as for your own retirement plans).

- In case your children inherit your retirement plan while they're too young to manage it.

- To make sure your heirs don't spend the money too quickly and lose the benefit of deferred taxation.

- If your child or another beneficiary has special needs.

- To make sure your spouse doesn't squander the funds or, upon death, pass them on to someone other than your children.

Unfortunately, what's already too complicated gets even more complicated when a trust becomes involved. And the SECURE Act passed at the end of 2019 made it still more complicated. To understand this, you will need to learn about four concepts: designated beneficiaries, eligible designated beneficiaries, conduit trusts and accumulation trusts.

DESIGNATED BENEFICIARIES AND ELIGIBLE DESIGNATED BENEFICIARIES

Prior to passage of the SECURE Act, for a beneficiary of an IRA or 401(k) plan to receive the benefits of an inherited IRA or a spousal IRA that permit them to spread withdrawals out through the rest of her life, she had to be a "designated" beneficiary. Now, anyone inheriting an IRA from someone dying on or after January 1, 2020, must withdraw the full account by the end of the 10th year after the owner's death unless she qualifies as an "eligible designated beneficiary." Only the following beneficiaries receive this designation:

- Spouses

- Minor children (until they reach the age of majority)

- Permanently disabled or chronically ill individuals

- Beneficiaries who are less than 10 years younger than the deceased owner

If any of these eligible designated beneficiaries or a trust for their sole benefit during their lives inherits an IRA, the IRA can be withdrawn under the required minimum distribution (RMD) rules that applied to all IRAs of people dying before the end of 2019. Other designated beneficiaries—which are other individuals or qualifying trusts—must withdraw the tax-deferred funds within 10 years. If there is no designated beneficiary, the funds must be withdrawn within five years—in all of these cases, accelerating the realization of income and payment of taxes.

A charity can never be a designated beneficiary and must withdraw all funds within five years of the donor's death, but this is not a problem since the charity will not be taxed on these withdrawals.

TRUSTS AS DESIGNATED BENEFICIARIES

Matters get more complicated, however, when a trust is involved. In order to qualify as a designated beneficiary, the trust must meet the following requirements:

- It must be valid under state law.

- It must be irrevocable or become irrevocable upon the grantor's death, which is the case with revocable trusts.

- The ultimate beneficiaries of the trust must be identifiable. You can say "my children," since anyone should be able to figure out who they are, but you cannot say "it's up to my trustee," since then one can't know who the trustee will choose.

- None of the ultimate beneficiaries can be a charity (or other non-person), since a charity cannot be a "designated" beneficiary.

- The trust documentation must be provided to the IRA custodian (the financial institution) by the October 31st following the year in which the owner died. Trust documentation includes the trust document, a list of the current and contingent beneficiaries, and a certification by the trustee that all of the above requirements have been met.

These requirements do not seem so hard to satisfy. But keep reading—determining the ultimate beneficiaries of the trust can be difficult.

CONDUIT OR "SEE THROUGH" TRUST

The easiest way to make sure a trust works (to preserve a withdrawal period based on the beneficiary's status, from 10 or more years up to their lifetime, rather than requiring withdrawal within 5 years of the original owner's death) is to make it a *conduit*. A conduit requires that all RMDs coming *into* the trust for eligible designated beneficiaries be distributed *out* from the trust each year to a named beneficiary or several named beneficiaries.

If the trust provides that all of the income must be paid to a single person, such as a surviving spouse, the annual RMDs will be based on her life expectancy. If it provides that the income must be distributed to a number of different beneficiaries, then the trust may well not qualify for the lifetime distribution scheme and therefore be subject to the new 10-year rule. Also, don't include a charity as an income beneficiary, since a charity is not a designated beneficiary and its inclusion will disqualify the trust entirely, requiring that all retirement funds be withdrawn within 5 years.

If your plan includes an existing conduit trust for someone other than your spouse or one of the other eligible designated beneficiaries named above, you need to reconsider it due to passage of the

SECURE Act. Prior to 2020, you may have felt comfortable with a trust providing that all the RMDs be taken and distributed to the beneficiaries each year when such would be relatively small, but now that the funds must be liquidated within 10 years of your death, you may no longer want those funds to be distributed and the trust terminated that quickly.

There may well be reasons you would want the retirement funds to stay in trust, even if they are no longer tax deferred. For estate tax reasons, you may want the trust to grow in value. You may not want one or more beneficiaries to have control over the funds because you don't think they will spend them wisely. Or, in the case of someone receiving public benefits, the distributions would make him ineligible with potentially drastic consequences. You may be concerned about creditor protection. For all of these reasons you may opt for an accumulation trust, described below, rather than a conduit trust.

ACCUMULATION TRUST

An accumulation trust continues to take the required RMDs for the IRA it contains, but it does not require those RMDs to be fully disbursed annually. Instead, the trustee has discretion over whether, when, and how much to distribute to beneficiaries.

With such trusts, in determining whether all beneficiaries qualify as designated and as eligible under the SECURE Act, the IRS will look to those beneficiaries named to receive the ultimate trust distribution. So, if your trust says it will continue for the life of your spouse and that the remainder will go to your children, the IRS will look to make sure that each child is identifiable. Presumably, your spouse (except in some second marriages) will be older than your children and RMDs will be based on her life expectancy. If the trust says that it will continue until all of your children have passed away and that then, everything will be distributed to your grandchildren, this is okay so long as at least one grandchild is living at your death. That works because the oldest grandchild is identifiable.

However, if all of the potential beneficiaries cannot be identified upon your death, or a charity is a potential beneficiary, that could disqualify the trust, requiring all retirement plans to be liquidated within 5 years of death. In addition, under the SECURE Act, even if one beneficiary does not qualify as eligible, the retirement plan will be subject to the 10-year rule. So, if your beneficiary qualifies as eligible, such as your spouse or a child with a disability, he should be the sole beneficiary during his life. Even including your children as possible beneficiaries during your spouse's life, or your child's children during his life, will subject the trust to the 10-year rule.

In short, it's much easier to use a conduit trust, but you may need to use an accumulation trust in situations where you do not want the mandatory IRA distributions distributed outright to the beneficiary. This can be the case under the following circumstances:

- In a second marriage, when you do not want all of the RMD funds to go to the surviving spouse, but you do want them available to him if needed.

- For tax reasons, when you do not want the RMD funds in the surviving spouse's or your children's taxable estates. (The latter will apply to very few people.)

- When the beneficiaries are minors or too young to responsibly handle the funds.

- When you would like to protect the RMDs as well as the principal from the reach of the beneficiaries' creditors.

- In the case of special needs trusts when, either for financial management purposes or to maintain eligibility for public benefits, the RMDs should not be distributed directly to the beneficiary.

While accumulation trusts continue to preserve retirement assets under the SECURE Act, they can also create higher taxes in two ways. First, when RMDs are withdrawn and distributed right out to the designated beneficiary, they are taxed to that beneficiary at their income tax rate. Individual tax rates are usually lower than trust tax rates. But if the IRA must be liquidated within 10 years, the trustee will be less likely to distribute it completely, and more of the distributions will be taxed at trust rates. In addition, the accelerated withdrawals will result in the realization of higher annual income for the trust, pushing the trust into higher tax brackets.

OTHER ALTERNATIVES

Given the complications of the SECURE Act, of accumulation trusts and the potential that they could be disqualified by mistake, we often try to avoid their use. For instance, if parents have one child with special needs and two who do not need the same protection, we may discuss having the retirement plans go to the two who do not need a trust with non-retirement funds going into the special needs trust. Of course, this can make it more difficult to make everyone's share of the estate equal, especially if the retirement plans constitute a large portion of the parents' estate. In addition, in the wake of the SECURE Act, it can make sense to reverse this advice since the children without special needs will be subject to the 10-year rule. For tax purposes, it may make sense to have the retirement plans go to the special needs trust for the child with the disability. In such cases, we will draft special needs trusts designed as accumulation trusts. (Then, we often have the problem of explaining the somewhat arcane provisions in the trusts as well as our higher fees for creating such a complicated plan, but we do the best we can.)

A case in our office illustrates this point. Our clients have two daughters—one quite high functioning and one facing a number of mental health and emotional difficulties. The first daughter does not need her money and the second one does but can't manage it herself. In addition, she may ultimately depend on public benefits that could be jeopardized if she were to receive RMDs directly. To further complicate matters, neither daughter has nor is likely to have children, so identifiable beneficiaries of an accumulation trust cannot be named. As a result, the parents (with our advice) decided to create a single trust for the two daughters and to not worry about stretching the RMDs. This will mean that all of their retirement funds will have to be withdrawn and taxes paid on them within five years of the death of the surviving parent. But we hope that this will be many years in the future and that by then the bulk of the retirement funds will have been spent down for their main purpose—the parents' retirement.

CHAPTER 19
TRUSTS FOR GRANDCHILDREN

While a number of the trusts described so far may be for the benefit of grandchildren as well as for children, some grandparents choose to create specific trusts for their grandchildren—in large part because they don't want them to have wait until the death of members of the intervening generation to receive the bounty of their grandparents' love. Often these are "pot" trusts, with the funds available to any and all grandchildren to be disbursed evenly or unevenly at the trustee's discretion.

These trusts also are more likely than others to have a stated purpose, for instance to pay for education, travel, summer camp, a downpayment for a house, or weddings. The idea, generally, is that these trusts are not meant to pay for basic costs of living, but for extras that will enhance the grandchildren's lives.

Grandparents can fund trusts for their grandchildren with a specific dollar amount or a share of their estate. I'm a fan of funding these trusts as if the trust were an additional child for purposes of dividing up the estate. Here's how that works: If you have two children, you would divide your estate three ways with one share each going to your children and one share to the grandchildren's trust. If you have three children, you would divide your estate four ways, with a quarter going to each of your children and a quarter going to the grandchildren's trust. And so on.

Use of the grandchildren's trust can satisfy some of the purposes of family protection trusts described in Chapter 15 without tying up assets for the next generation. In order for family protection trusts to work, they must limit the next generation's access to the funds they hold. Some children object to those restrictions, arguing that they can well manage their own funds and that it's demeaning to have to ask a trustee for funds. So, one solution is to give them their share of your estate outright, but to set some funds aside for the following generation through a grandchildren's trust to make sure at least these funds are protected for them in the event adverse circumstances befall their parents.

CHAPTER 20
PURPOSE TRUSTS

As discussed in Chapter 19 regarding grandchildren's trusts, trust distributions can be limited to prescribed purposes. Sometimes these are meant to support the grantor's values. In the description of grandchildren's trusts, we discussed trusts to support education, a down payment for a house, payment for weddings, or travel.

Trusts also may be used to motivate certain actions. For instance, a grantor may have somewhat ne'er-do-well offspring and want to encourage them to take on gainful employment. The trust might match their earnings. We had clients who did just that for their grandsons, but not their granddaughters. Their son had become a very observant Jew and joined a sect that valued the study of the Talmud above all else, but only by men, not women. The women's role was to work to support the family. These clients wanted to help their granddaughters and encourage their grandsons to go out and work. So the granddaughters received their shares of estate with no strings attached, but the grandsons could only receive a match to their earnings.

Some purposes, however, are barred by case law as against public policy. While it's okay to reward people for getting married by providing for a distribution upon marriage, it has been ruled as against public policy to limit such a distribution to marriages to others of the same race. No doubt, under current law, it would not be okay to provide for distributions in the case of opposite-sex marriages but not for same-sex marriages.

Other than for purposes deemed to be against public policy, trusts can be created to support just about any purposes. But the more unusual the purpose, the greater the risk that no distribution will be allowed. So, beware too much creativity.

CHAPTER 21

LIFE INSURANCE TRUSTS

Life insurance trusts have long been used as a way to shelter life insurance proceeds from being taxed in estates, though they are used less now with the estate tax threshold at $11.7 million (in 2021) than years ago when it was as low as $600,000. For those with potentially significant estates who are considering sheltering the proceeds from taxation through a trust, there are a few basic rules to review to understand how these work, including the so-called "Crummey" powers.

First, life insurance proceeds are not subject to *income* taxation. However, if owned by the decedent, they will be included in his estate for *estate* tax purposes. As mentioned, this is much less of a concern today than it was in past years, but it's still a concern for the very wealthy and those who live in states with lower estate tax thresholds. Further, more people will have taxable estates when the federal threshold gets cut by half in 2026. If that could include you, you might want to buy a policy now rather than then, when you'll be five years older and perhaps less insurable.

Second, life insurance on your life will be taxed only upon your death if you own the policy. If, instead, your children own the policy, it won't be taxed. However, before urging your children to purchase a policy on your life, you have to be confident that they can afford to pay the premiums and that the policy and its proceeds won't be at risk in the event they run into financial trouble, are sued, or get divorced—all the reasons for using a trust. You can always give your children the funds to pay the premiums, just so that the amount you give, along with any other gifts you make to them, does not exceed $15,000 a year (in 2021) each ($30,000 if your spouse is sharing in making the gifts). If you give them more, you'll have to file a gift tax return, using up some of your estate tax credit.

Third, you could also give your children a life insurance policy you already own, but make sure you don't do so on your deathbed. For tax purposes, your estate will include the proceeds of any policy you transfer within the three years before you die.

Fourth, often life insurance policies used in estate tax planning are very large, all the more reason individuals want to make sure they are well managed. Trusts permit them to put a trusted family member or professional in charge. A trust can also provide that a surviving spouse be the beneficiary during her life without the funds being included in her estate for tax purposes.

Here's where things get interesting (at least for lawyers) and complicated. If you have your life insurance in an irrevocable trust and you give the trust the funds necessary to pay the annual premiums, those transfers to the trust normally do not qualify for the $15,000 annual gift tax exclusion because the exclusion only applies to gifts to individuals, not to trusts.

So, fifth, this is where Crummey powers come in. It's a great name because implementing these powers is difficult, but they're named after the court case that authorized their use. Crummey powers in trusts are provisions that permit beneficiaries to withdraw transfers to the trust. Since the trust beneficiaries have this right, they are deemed to have received the transfers to the trust, even if they don't exercise their right to take the funds out (and they shouldn't exercise that right because then the trust wouldn't have sufficient funds to pay the life insurance premiums).

Here's how this typically works: Dad transfers $20,000 to the trust to pay the annual premiums. The trustee then sends a letter to son and daughter who are the ultimate beneficiaries of the trust, reporting that the funds have been deposited and that they have 30 days to withdraw up to $10,000 each. Son and daughter throw away the letters with the rest of their junk mail. Thirty days later, the trustee pays the life insurance premiums.

Or, at least, that's how it's supposed to work. As often as not, no one follows these rules. Dad just pays the premiums directly, no money passes through the trust, and no notice goes to daughter and son. In that case, the life insurance proceeds may still be outside of dad's estate, but there will be a lot of cleanup necessary at his death to report the premium payments which are taxable gifts.

In addition, who would want to be the trustee for these trusts? It means taking on significant responsibility and the annual task of chasing after dad to get the premium funds and writing letters to daughter and son. How much is dad willing to pay for this administrative service? If the estate planning attorney has taken on this duty, will she remember to follow through every year, and does she really want to be worried about this task? Probably not. It works best in a law firm or accounting practice with many life insurance trusts where they can assign a staff member to administer all of them.

Based on my experience, unless you have a very large estate facing a significant estate tax, life insurance trusts are generally not worth the trouble.

CHAPTER 22
PET TRUSTS

Until relatively recently, you could not leave money to a trust to care for your pets. Fortunately, every state has now enacted laws authorizing the creation of trusts for pets, with Minnesota being the last to have done so. Yet most people do not include them in their estate plans, either assuming that their pets will pass away long before they do or that family and friends will simply step in to take care of them. And this is usually the case.

But if you do not have family or friends who are likely to step in, would like to compensate whoever does step up to the plate, or have exotic pets that require special care, you might want to make provisions for them in your estate plan. We once had clients who owned rare parrots and made arrangements for the often surprisingly long-lived birds to go to a particular sanctuary in the event the parrots outlived both owners.

The first thing to know about planning for pets is that they are treated like property so that through your will you can give them to whomever you choose, just like your other possessions. But first talk to the person or people you plan to name to make sure that they are ready to take on this responsibility.

The second factor to consider is that you cannot leave money directly to a pet. So, if you want to compensate the person taking care of your pet or pets or provide a fund to pay for expenses, such as for veterinarians, dog walkers, or people to care for the pets when the primary caregiver is traveling or otherwise unavailable, this can be done in one of two ways (or both). You can simply leave money to the caregiver with the understanding—whether explicit in your will or trust or through conversations with the caregiver—as to why you are making the gift. Or you can create a trust for the benefit of your pet.

There are several advantages to a pet trust. It makes certain sufficient money is available for whatever your pet's needs may be in the future and in case circumstances change so that your designated caregiver can no longer take care of your pet. It also permits you to leave specific instructions, such as providing for a romp in the dog park every day or a visit to the veterinarian at least twice a year. The disadvantage is simply that a trust, as opposed to a less formal arrangement, creates another level of planning and administrative cost. However, those pet owners who do not have a natural care system of friends and family in place generally find these costs to be more than justified by the reassurance that their pet will be cared for appropriately.

A further advantage of a pet trust is that it can go into effect during your life in the event of incapacity; the protections it provides do not have to wait until you pass away.

Some states also have statutory pet trusts: laws containing all of the trust provisions, which make these easier to set up and mean that the pet owner has fewer decisions to make about the trust terms. They can also use them, if they like their provisions, without hiring a lawyer to prepare the trust. Of course, for some people, the cost of setting up a tailored trust is not an undue burden.

In probably the most famous pet trust case, hotel heiress Leona Helmsley, who died in 2007, left $12 million for the benefit of her white Maltese, Trouble, and nothing to two of her four grandchildren. The court later reduced this amount to $2 million, determining that the extra $10 million was unnecessary. According to an article in *The New York Times*,when Trouble died in 2012, her annual expenses were about $190,000, the bulk of which—$100,000—went for security costs. Her guardian, the general manager of the Helmsley Sandcastle Hotel in Sarasota, Florida, received $60,000, and the balance of the expenses went for grooming, food, and veterinary costs.

A number of websites provide pet trust forms, including:

- **RocketLawyer**: www.rocketlawyer.com/document/pet-trust.rl#/
- **Lexis/Nexis:** www.lexisnexis.com/documents/ pdf/20090701050818_large.pdf
- **LegalZoom:** www.legalzoom.com/personal/estate-planning/ pet-protection-agreement-overview.html

  LegalZoom's form is actually a pet protection agreement between the pet owner and the appointed caregiver, rather than a trust. You can read more about this concept here (www.legalzoom.com/ knowledge/pet-protection). Legal/Zoom recommends using an attorney to create a more formal pet trust. The pet protection agreement could be entered into, along with the creation of the trust, with the agreement providing for care and the trust providing for payment of pet-related costs.

CHAPTER 23
NOMINEE TRUSTS

Nominee trusts or nominee realty trusts are primarily used in Massachusetts as a means to hold title to real estate without putting the names of the true owners on record at the registry of deeds. They're hybrid documents with characteristics of both trusts and agency agreements, the latter being more like a durable power of attorney through which one person names another as her agent to carry out tasks and responsibilities on her behalf.

The typical nominee trust names one or more trustees to hold title to real estate on behalf of and at the direction of one or more individuals or entities—other trusts or corporations—listed on a separate schedule of beneficiaries. The schedule of beneficiaries is not recorded at the registry of deeds, so the identity of the underlying owners is kept confidential. In addition, the ownership can be changed without the requirement of recording a new deed at the registry. This can facilitate gifts over time.

The use of nominee trusts grew in Massachusetts because the state was late to adopt a recording rule common in other states. Until relatively recently, if Massachusetts property was placed in trust in Massachusetts, the entire trust had to be recorded at the registry. This was undesirable for many reasons. The trust could be 20 to 30 pages long, increasing the recording cost. It could contain many elements the grantor and beneficiaries would prefer to keep private. Any amendment would have to be recorded as well.

In other states, and now in Massachusetts as well, when property is transferred to a trust, all that needs to be recorded is a certificate of trustee detailing the name of the trust and trustees.

USES OF NOMINEE TRUSTEES

Nevertheless, nominee trusts continue to be used in Massachusetts in certain circumstances, including the following:

- There's no underlying trust, but the owners want to keep their identities private.

- The owners want to convey property interests over time without recording new deeds. For instance, parents may want to transfer ownership of a vacation house to their children over time without exceeding the $15,000 annual gift tax exclusion. They can do this by amending the schedule of beneficiaries each year to increase their children's interests while reducing their own.

- Having too many owners on the title to property can be cumbersome. For instance, a parent may create a life estate by conveying the remainder interest in her home to her four children while retaining her life interest. If subsequently, she were to decide to sell or mortgage the property, she would need all four children to sign off on the transaction; she could be prevented from moving forward if one opposed the plan or was unavailable or incapacitated. A nominee trust would allow her to move forward if a majority of her children agreed. Further, a nominee trust helps reduce difficulties if an owner dies: his interest will pass as set out in his estate plan, whether he has title to the property in his name or has an interest in the property through the nominee trust. However, if he has title in his name, his estate will have to be probated in order to clear title to the property. This is not the case if title is held by a nominee trust.

PROBLEMS WITH NOMINEE TRUSTS

In our practice, we've come across two problems with nominee trusts. First, quite often no one can locate the schedule of beneficiaries. Clients often don't understand how the trusts work and why a schedule of beneficiaries is important. The lawyer who drew up the documents may or may not still be practicing and able to find the document in his files. And, of course, the schedule of beneficiaries is not recorded at the registry of deeds, since doing so would defeat the purpose of using the nominee trust in the first place. In such cases, we usually ask the clients for their understanding of the underlying ownership of the property and draw up a new schedule of beneficiaries consistent with their memory. For obvious reasons, this workaround is far from perfect.

The second problem we've seen is misuse of nominee trusts by attorneys. This occurs in two ways. First, while the trust might be titled "nominee realty trust," some attorneys add elements to the document that are typically found in standard trusts. Then, despite the trust's name, the trust moves from an agency agreement more towards a standard trust. The result is a hybrid with its legal effect somewhat unclear, and it gets into the nitty-gritty that only a lawyer can love.

The second departure from norms may or may not create legal problems but should still be avoided. Some attorneys become creative with the schedules of beneficiaries. The most common form of this is for the schedule to say who will receive the property interest upon the current beneficiary's death. For instance, it might say that each of four children owns an interest in the family house and that each child's interest will pass to her children upon her death. It isn't totally clear legally what this means. Is this enforceable? What happens if the property is sold—must the proceeds be held for the grandchildren? Does the grandchild have a say in whether the property is sold? What if a grandchild dies before a child?

In short, it's much better to keep it simple. The trustees of a nominee trust must act on behalf of the beneficiaries. The beneficiaries, along with their percentage interests, are named on the schedule of beneficiaries. If an attorney or client wants to get fancy, use a standard trust.

CHAPTER 24
GRITS, GRATS, GRUTS, QPRTS, AND QDOTS

There's a bowl of alphabet soup's worth of acronyms for specific trusts used for tax planning. Each of these trusts can have significant potential tax benefits for those with taxable estates, but also significant drawbacks, outlined in this chapter.

In addition to QTIP trusts described in Chapter 11 for marital estate tax planning, there are GRITs, GRATs, GRUTs, QPRTs, and QDOTs. The first four, which all involve leveraging current gifts while retaining an interest in the property, have fallen by the wayside, with estates under $11.7 million for individuals and $23.4 million for married couples (in 2021) not being subject to federal estate taxation. But they may come back into play for the merely wealthy as opposed to just the extremely wealthy when the current estate tax thresholds expire on January 1, 2026, falling back to half their levels on that date.

GRITS, GRATS, AND GRUTS

Grantor retained income trusts (GRITs), grantor retained annuity trusts (GRATs), and grantor retained unitrusts (GRUTs) are all variations on the same theme. They all permit you to remove property from your taxable estate while continuing to receive a benefit from it. Depending on the trust, you might receive the income produced by the property (from a GRIT), a specific dollar amount each year (from a GRAT), or a percentage of the value of the property (from a GRUT). An example should better explain how this works.

Let's assume you have a taxable estate and you transfer a $1 million stock portfolio into a trust retaining one of the interests described above. That transfer will be a completed gift and, as a result, you will have to file a gift tax return using up some of the $11.7 million you're allowed to give away free of estate and gift taxation. Your first response may be to question how this reduces taxes, since you're using up some of what you can give away tax free in any case. It works for three reasons.

First, while you're giving away $1 million, your gift tax return will report a smaller amount because of your retained interest. Depending on your age and the retained interest you choose, the discount may be smaller or larger. For example, while you might remove $1 million from your estate, your gift tax return might report a gift of just $700,000. The amount of the discount is determined by complicated formulas that have been approved by the IRS.

Second, any growth in the value of the property will occur outside of your estate. If you live for another 20 years, your $1 million stock portfolio may double or triple in value to $2 million or $3 million. All that growth will be outside your estate; so while your gift might use up $1 million (or less with the discount) of your unified estate and gift tax credit, you will have removed substantially more from being taxed upon your death. At the same time, you will continue to benefit from some or all of the income produced by the transferred property.

Third, we are currently in a unique time period that further enhances the value of these trusts. As mentioned above, the current estate and gift tax thresholds are slated to be cut in half at the beginning of 2026. The IRS has issued guidance saying that taxable gifts made before the end of 2025 will count against the current estate tax thresholds and will not be counted against the lower ones in place if the taxpayer dies in 2026 or later. Let's say, for example, that you have an estate totaling $10 million and you're concerned about what will happen when the estate tax threshold drops from its current level of $11.7 million to approximately half that amount in 2026. Since the option of dying before 2026 is unappealing, you could give away $5 million before the end of 2025. This would use up a part of your $11.7 million estate and gift tax credit, but it would not count against the lower credit in place beginning in 2026. So, then you would have $5 million remaining, below that lower threshold.

In considering taking these steps to reduce estate taxes, you have to take into account the potentially adverse effect they may have on capital gains taxes. Those who inherit property receive a so-called "step-up" in basis. The basis in the property is adjusted to the value of the property on the decedent's date of death. On the other hand, those who receive property as a gift receive it with the same basis as the donor.

Going back to the example of the $1 million stock portfolio. Let's assume you inherited this portfolio from your parents and at that time its value was $200,000. That is the basis in the portfolio. If you were to sell all the stock, you would have to pay taxes on the gain of $800,000. Your tax would be approximately 25% (the exact percentage depending on your income and state taxes) for a tax of approximately $200,000. If you were to give the portfolio to your children, whether outright or through a trust, and they sold it for the same amount, they would have to pay the same tax. If, instead, they inherited the portfolio from you, the basis in the stock would be adjusted to its value on your date of death. If that were still $1 million and they sold it at that time, they would save the $200,000 in taxes on capital gains.

Let's push this example a bit further by assuming that by the time of your death the portfolio has increased in value to $2 million. Then, if your children had received the property as a gift and they sold it, the gain would be $1.8 million with a tax of approximately $450,000, a tax that would have been completely avoided if your children had received the property by inheritance rather than as a gift.

As you can see, calculating the potential benefits of using a GRIT, GRAT, or GRUT depends both on some complicated calculations, the type of property being transferred, and assumptions about both future tax policies and the likelihood that property will be sold. Such calculations must be carried out by experienced tax professionals. Our firm, in fact, has never prepared one of these trusts. We've referred the few clients we've met with who might consider this estate tax planning strategy to law firms with specialties in sophisticated tax planning.

QPRTS

A qualified personal residence trust, or QPRT, is a variation on the theme of GRITs, GRATs, and GRUTs. While they all can hold real estate, QPRTs are designed only for the client's personal residence or vacation home.

Similar to the trusts described above, QPRTs involve transferring the home to the trust but retaining certain rights—in this case the right to live in the house rather than an income interest. Typically, that right lasts for a specific number of years: the longer the span, the greater the gift's discount. However, there's a risk with a lengthy right to live in the house because, if the grantor dies before the right to live in the property has expired, the house remains in her estate, eliminating the tax benefit for which the QPRT was created.

Let's assume for example that you wish to transfer your property to a QPRT and decide on a 5-year term, a smaller discount than if you chose a 10-year term, but making it more likely that you will outlive the term. You may very well then ask what happens after five years when you no longer have the right under the terms of the trust to live in the property. You don't want to be kicked out of your home. The answer is that when you execute the QPRT you will also sign a lifetime lease or use and occupancy agreement giving you the right to continue to use and live in the property. You'll have to pay fair market rent to the trust or to your children directly if the trust is structured to end at the completion of its term. This will be taxable income to them to the extent it exceeds their expenses in maintaining the property, but it permits you to transfer additional funds to them without having to file a gift tax return each year.

QPRTs have the same problem of GRITs, GRATs, and GRUTs in that your children will receive the house with your basis rather than with one that is stepped up at your death. Whether or not they plan to sell the property after your death must be considered in the calculations made to determine whether a QPRT is worth the trouble and expense of setting it up and following its rules. It may be more worth it for a vacation house the family never intends to sell.

QDOTS

QDOTs are qualified domestic trusts used for taxpayers whose spouses are not U.S. citizens. This is because the estate tax marital deduction does not apply to non-citizen spouses.

Under the federal tax code, there is no tax on gifts or estates going to U.S. citizen spouses, no matter how large your estate may be. So, for instance, if your estate were worth $100 million, you could give it all to your spouse with no estate tax due. (The fact that this exemption was not allowed same-sex couples led the Supreme Court to bar restrictions on same-sex marriages nationwide.)

However, this rule does not apply to non-citizen spouses. They are treated like any other recipient of your estate. In terms of *lifetime* gifts, things are even more complicated. While you can give non-spouses only $15,000 a year without having to file a gift tax return, you can give your non-citizen spouse $157,000 (in 2021) without filing a gift tax return. (The reality is that very few people observe these rules during their lives.) These rules apply whether or not the taxpayer is a U.S. citizen. What matters is only the citizenship of the recipient spouse.

For most taxpayers, these rules are irrelevant since you can still give away $11.7 million to your non-citizen spouse estate tax free, just like your gifts to any non-spouse. However, more estates could be subject to estate taxation when the thresholds drop in half in 2026 and some states have significantly lower estate tax thresholds. If you have a non-citizen spouse and either have an estate greater than $5 million or live in a state with its own estate tax, you will want to consider creating a QDOT.

QDOTs are designed similarly to QTIP and marital trusts described in Chapter 11 to shelter the funds left by the first spouse to die so they are not taxed upon the death of the surviving spouse. They are somewhat more restrictive than typical marital or QTIP trusts; and if they hold more than $2 million, you must name a U.S. bank as a trustee.

To see how this works, let's assume that you and your spouse each have estates of $4 million. You can leave everything to each other and there would be no estate tax upon the death of the first spouse to pass away. Then the surviving spouse would have $8 million and as a non-U.S. citizen she would not qualify for portability (also described in Chapter 11 on estate tax planning). If she then passes away in 2026 or later, her estate would be taxed on the excess over the threshold in place at that time. Perhaps as much as $2 million would be subject to a 40% tax, resulting in $800,000 of taxes. This could be avoided if the first spouse's estate went into a QDOT, which would keep it out of the surviving spouse's taxable estate. These become useful for smaller estates for those living in states with lower estate tax thresholds. As of this writing, Massachusetts and Oregon still have $1 million thresholds, meaning that QDOTs could reduce estate taxes for the heirs of any couple in those states who together own assets of more than $1 million if one or both are non-citizens. While we've never created GRITs, GRATs, GRUTs, or QPRTs in our practice, we have created QDOTs for certain clients.

Finally, be aware that if the surviving non-citizen spouse moves out of the United States after the death of her spouse and she doesn't remove all her funds and property from the country, her estate could be subject to a draconian estate tax. The estates of non-resident non-citizens with property in the United States are taxed above a $60,000 threshold instead of $11.7 million. It's an odd law since it creates a very strong incentive for non-resident, non-citizens to move their assets out of the country.

SECTION 3
AIDS IN PLANNING

CHAPTER 25

DIY OR GET AN ATTORNEY?

So, now that you know all you need to know about trusts, should you create your own using one of the online do-it-yourself programs available, or work with an attorney?

The online programs have the advantage of lower cost and often easier implementation, since you can fill out the forms in the privacy of your own home at whatever time of day or night works for you. On the other hand, the programs may not answer your questions, guide you on difficult choices, take state differences into account, or keep you moving along towards completing your plan. (In terms of answering questions, LegalZoom does offer consultations with attorneys at a very reasonable added cost.)

My conclusion is that an online program should suffice if your goal is to:

- execute a revocable trust to avoid probate,
- provide for asset management in the event of your incapacity, and
- provide for your minor children in the event of your untimely demise.

However, you're better off working with an estate planning attorney for any of the following reasons:

- Special needs planning, whether for yourself, a child, or grandchild
- A taxable estate, federally or in your state
- Asset protection planning, whether for yourself or for your heirs
- Second (or subsequent) marriage or relationship
- Blended family
- Long-term care planning
- No trusted family member or close friend to serve as successor trustee
- Real estate in another state or country
- Non–U.S. citizen spouse
- Need for answers to legal questions
- Need to understand existing legal documents
- You're just not getting it done

CHAPTER 26
FINDING THE RIGHT ATTORNEY

If you decide to work with an attorney in crafting your trust or trusts rather than using an online program, the next step is to find the right attorney. I would recommend taking the following steps:

ASK AROUND

The best way to start is through word of mouth. If your family, friends or trusted advisors—such as financial planners, accountants, or attorneys who specialize in other fields—recommend someone, that's a significant vote of confidence. Both professional and non-professional recommendations are important. Unlike the attorney's peers who may know her professional reputation, former clients or those who have worked with the attorney will know whether she's good to work with, returns phone calls, readily answers questions, and gets the job done.

CHECK THE INTERNET

Once you have one or more candidates, check out their websites. This will give you more information about their background, specialization, and experience and provide a feel for who they are as people.

CALL

Call the office to see how they work. Do they charge hourly or set a flat fee? Do you need to come into the office, or can you meet by videoconference? Is there a charge for the initial meeting? If they couldn't take your call immediately, did they call you back in a timely manner? By calling, you should get an idea about how the attorney and his office work.

INTERVIEW

Whether or not attorneys charge for the initial consultation, they'll usually get on the phone with you for at least a few minutes to discuss your situation and goals. That will give you the opportunity to get a feel for the attorney and see if there's a good fit.

CHECK THEIR DISCIPLINE RECORD

It's worth checking attorneys' records with your state's licensing organization. Over the course of a long career, anyone could have difficulties with one or more clients; but for it to rise to the level of being disciplined—whether with an admonition or suspension—

means that the matter was serious. While everyone can learn from their mistakes or go through a rough patch, if you have a choice between two attorneys, one who has been disciplined and one who hasn't, go with the one who has not been disciplined.

FEES

For most clients, cost is an important factor—both the cost of the initial meeting and for the work involved. Estate planning attorneys are more likely to charge for initial consultation than lawyers in many other fields because the meeting is usually one where the work actually begins. Getting to know the clients, their situation, their family, and their goals is a big part of the estate planning process. It's hard not to answer legal questions and begin talking about estate planning solutions. Many lawyers don't want to invest in doing so without charging at least a nominal fee. And they don't want to be put in the position of "hiding the ball" and trying to sell their services. On the other hand, other attorneys are comfortable offering these services at no charge, assuming the clients will hire them to do the subsequent work; and if a few don't, so be it.

Estate planning attorneys are also more likely than many other attorneys to do work for a flat fee rather than hourly. After the initial meeting, if the attorney and the clients have decided on a course of action, the attorney should have a pretty good idea of what work will be involved and be able to quote a specific fee.

It can be difficult to price shop because attorneys will be reluctant to quote a fee or provide an estimate until they have had the initial meeting and have a pretty good idea of the work involved. To get two or more quotes and make sure you're comparing apples to apples, you would really have to go through more than one initial consultation.

But that said, if you describe generally what you need, attorneys can provide at least a range of what the charges may be.

In comparing fees charged by different attorneys or law firms, to some extent you get what you pay for. But the market is far from efficient or transparent. Sometimes the attorney with more knowledge and better service will charge less than the one with less experience and worse service. Again, word of mouth can go a long way towards letting you know the quality of the representation you will receive.

ORGANIZATIONS

Many estate planning attorneys are members of one or more organizations, especially if they specialize in a specific practice area. Some organizations have strict membership rules and others admit everyone who applies. Below are listed some of the prime organizations for estate planning attorneys. Membership in them is at least an indication of their interest in the field and commitment to staying abreast of new developments. But membership is not a guarantee of the attorney's competence and responsiveness. Nor does non-membership mean that the attorney does not have sufficient expertise in the particular specialty. It's just one more factor to consider. If, for instance, an elder law attorney is not a member of the National Academy of Elder Law Attorneys, you can certainly ask him why not. His answer may well be that he's a member of the elder law section of his state bar and that he finds the local information it provides more relevant to his practice than the national information provided by NAELA.

American College of Trust and Estate Counsel. www.actec.org. This group is generally for attorneys representing larger estates for whom sophisticated tax planning is necessary. Membership is by invitation only.

National Academy of Elder Law Attorneys. www.naela.org. As its name indicates, this group consists of elder law attorneys around the country. Any elder law attorney may join. It has chapters in a number of states.

ElderLawAnswers. www.elderlawanswers.com. This organization of elder law attorneys provides consumers with a rich database of information about elder law issues on its website. It provides its members with marketing tools, including a listing on its site and a monthly e-letter that members can send to their clients and referral sources. Membership is open to all elder law attorneys with at least three years of experience. Full disclosure: I founded the site and organization.

Special Needs Alliance. www.specialneedsalliance.org. Membership in this organization of special needs planning attorneys is by invitation only.

Academy of Special Needs Planners. www.specialneedsanswers. com. This organization includes financial planners and trust administrators as well as attorneys. Any attorney with at least three years' experience in special needs planning may join. Full disclosure: I co-founded this organization, in part because, along with the other co-founders, I was not invited to join the Special Needs Alliance.

CHAPTER 27
GUIDING YOUR TRUSTEE

Trustees have a lot of power over property in trust: how it may be maintained and invested, and how liquid assets are distributed to or withheld from beneficiaries. In most cases, trustees are chosen because the trust grantor has confidence in their judgment and faith that they share values. In practice, trust grantors rarely provide guidance and trustees rarely request it. Trustees simply apply their own values in making decisions. This usually works reasonably well, but it could work better if grantors better communicated their goals for the trust and wishes for how the funds are distributed to beneficiaries.

SAMPLE QUESTIONS FOR GRANTORS

While every trust is different, here are some examples of the types of questions and level of detail that a grantor may want to leave guidance on for the trustee.

Let's assume you're creating a trust for your minor children and naming your brother as trustee. The trust provides that if you and your spouse both pass away, your brother will hold the trust as a single fund until your youngest child reaches age 25. After that, the trust will be divided into separate shares for each of your children with the funds in each share being distributed to them in thirds when they reach ages 25, 30 and 35. In the meantime, it will be up to your brother how to distribute the funds remaining in trust for the benefit of each of your children.

You could just leave all decisions up to your brother's judgment, or you could provide him some guidance on how you would like him to spend the money. Here are some questions he might ask:

1. While the children are minors, should the funds be spent freely to pay for summer camp, private school, travel, etc.?

2. If the children are living with another family member or friend, how should living costs be covered?

3. Once the children go off to college, assuming they do, does it matter how expensive their schools are? In other words, if one child goes to an expensive private college and the other goes to a less expensive public university or does not go to college at all, should their shares of the trust be equalized?

4. What about graduate school?

5. Should the trust pay for travel if I [your brother] determine it is educational or simply broadens the mind?

6. Should it pay for a car? If so, how luxurious?

7. Once the children get older, should the trust pay for a house, or at least for a down payment?

8. Should it pay for a wedding? If so, how extravagant?

9. And if things don't work out so well, should the trust pay for lawyers for a divorce?

10. What if one or more children are having trouble finding work; how much support should the trust pay? How should the trustee distinguish between providing necessary support during a recession or time of illness and creating a disincentive to work?

11. Should the trust pay for health insurance?

12. What if the child wants to use trust funds to make a charitable or political contribution?

For many trusts, a big question is this: How should the trustee balance the interests of current beneficiaries as opposed to future ones? For instance, what if you're in a second marriage and you want to provide for your spouse but also for your children from your first marriage? You may want the trust to support your spouse as needed but not want it to be entirely drained doing so. Trust documents often provide some vague guidance saying that the trust funds may be used "as necessary" to support the surviving spouse "in the manner to which they are accustomed." But they're usually unclear about what this means. What was their living standard at the time of the first spouse's death? How much should the trustee investigate the surviving spouse's other resources? Is this even what you want? You may have been able to live a somewhat extravagant life based on your combined income and resources. Do you really want to support that lifestyle when you're no longer part of it, to the detriment of your children? Maybe yes, maybe no. But whatever your wishes are, they should be communicated to your trustee.

SPECIAL NEEDS TRUSTS

By definition, the beneficiaries of special needs trusts have special needs. The trustees need to know a lot about the beneficiaries, what disability they may be suffering, what treatment, care, or assistance they may be receiving, and the wishes of the grantors. Parents often provide fundamental care and support for their children with special needs for their entire lives and are rightfully concerned that no one will be able to provide the same level of support and advocacy when they're no longer able to fill that role. They need to empower their trustees to fill in as best they can.

Special needs planners often advise their clients to write a "memorandum of intent" for the trustee to provide information about the beneficiary and the goals of the trust. And they advise their clients to review these letters annually to make sure they're up to date.

The Academy of Special Needs Attorneys advises clients to include:

1. The names and contact information of all family members, physicians, therapists, and others who provide support.

2. All financial support the beneficiary may receive, including any governmental programs.

3. Information about current living arrangements and future plans.

4. Information about any programs the beneficiary may be participating in and services she may receive.

5. Personal preferences for everything from clothing to recreation to food.

6. Information about the beneficiary's abilities and needs.

Within each category, the list of items is quite extensive. It is available on the Academy's website at www.specialneedsanswers.com.

LETTERS OF INTENT

The Appendix contains four questionnaires for guiding your trustee: the first two for special needs trusts, the third for family protection trusts, and the last regarding real estate owned by the trust.

CHAPTER 28
CONCLUSION

As you can see, there's a lot to learn about trusts, both how they can be used and their operation or management. All of this can get complicated. But I'd like to end with a few words of reassurance if you have been appointed trustee of a trust.

First, if you have any questions, start by reading the trust. It's a roadmap that lays out how it should be operated, what distributions the trustee must or may make, and the standards for making those distributions. Unfortunately, some trusts are written more in legalese than in regular English, which can make them hard to understand. In addition, they include a lot of boilerplate that's included either for tax reasons or to take into account an unusual circumstance that someone encountered at some time during the past century. So, if you still have questions, unfortunately, you'll have to ask an attorney who understands the strange language of trusts or may have encountered the unusual situation for which some of the boilerplate was drafted.

Second, if you're a trustee, read the trust at least once a year. No one's memory is perfect, and no one stays the same—neither the trustee nor the beneficiary. What seemed irrelevant last year may be quite relevant this year.

Third, follow the basic requirements of trust management: staying in touch with beneficiaries so you know their needs, investing trust assets prudently, sending annual accounts to beneficiaries, hiring professional legal or accounting assistance as necessary, and (again) reading the trust. If you take these steps, someone might question your judgment, but you won't be held liable for malfeasance or neglect. We're all allowed to make bad decisions, whether bad in the opinion of others or in retrospect. It's the failure to carry out the duties of trustee that can get us in trouble.

Fourth, if for whatever reason you can't carry out the duties as trustee, whether due to time constraints, illness, or a breakdown of communication with one or more beneficiaries, either hire a professional co-trustee or resign. A professional trustee such as a bank, trust company, or attorney, can take care of most of the heavy lifting. It can also act as a bulwark against complaints from beneficiaries, almost "good cop, bad cop." You can tell them that you understand their wish to buy a Ferrari and would go along with that, but the independent trustee won't let you. And remember, this is not a lifetime appointment. If it isn't working, resign and give the headache to someone else.

Finally, if you have questions not answered by this book or by your professional advisors, ask me. You can do so at www.AskHarry.info.

ACKNOWLEDGMENTS

Much of what I've learned about the role of trustee has been through acting as trustee or co-trustee for dozens of trusts over the years. So, first, I need to thank my clients for having sufficient confidence to place me in this role of utmost responsibility. I hope I have carried out the duties to their satisfaction and to that of their beneficiaries.

Two people have been essential to my serving as trustee: Lawrence B. Cohen and Eugenia Andrade. As my co-trustee on many trusts, Larry has taught me how to balance both present and future needs of beneficiaries while meeting all the legal requirements of the trusts. Always taking a practical approach, rather than one that puts form over function, Larry is the quintessential trustee.

Eugenia has been the person in our office who makes sure we take all the necessary steps as trustees, whether paying bills, making disbursements, filing tax returns, or sending out annual accounts. She also serves as the primary contact with our trust beneficiaries and as such knows their circumstances and allows us to serve their needs and fulfill the grantors' goals in creating the trusts in the first place. Eugenia makes the proverbial trains run on time.

ABOUT THE AUTHOR

A passionate advocate for seniors, individuals with special needs, and their families, Harry S. Margolis has been practicing elder law and estate planning for more than 30 years. Through his initial firm, ElderLawServices, and his current firm, Margolis & Bloom, he has helped thousands of clients pay for long-term care, grapple with the incapacity of a family member, and secure the futures of their children and grandchildren.

Harry edited *The ElderLaw Report*, a monthly newsletter for attorneys, for three decades. He has been selected as a fellow of both the National Academy of Elder Law Attorneys and the American College of Trust & Estate Counsel. He has also been named a "Super Lawyer" every year since 2005, and in some years has been recognized as among the top 100 "Super Lawyers" in Massachusetts and New England.

The founder of the websites ElderLawAnswers.com and SpecialNeedsAnswers.com, Harry answers consumer estate planning questions online at AskHarry.info, reflecting his commitment to empowering everyday people with the knowledge they need to achieve the best legal solutions. More recently, Harry has begun exploring how Baby Boomers have shaped the United States in a blog at okayboomer.substack.com.

He is an elected town meeting member in Brookline, Massachusetts, where he lives with his wife, Susan, Cola, their old dog of uncertain breed, and, having returned home due to the pandemic, his 20-something twins, Maya and Jeremy. He loves biking and traveling, which have been rather curtailed during the pandemic, thus this new book.

APPENDIX

GUIDANCE TO TRUSTEE OF SPECIAL NEEDS TRUST

MEMORANDUM OF INTENT

A Memorandum of intent is a personal letter from you to the people who will care for your child when you no longer can. It supplements your estate plan by providing information that is not appropriate to include in your special needs trust because:

- it changes over time,

- it is your wish but not a legal requirement, or

- it is too lengthy and detailed to include in the trust.

Begin by filling out the easiest or most applicable parts of your Memorandum of Intent that you have the answers to right now. Then, over time, you can add to the document, filling in missing information and refining your wishes and direction. Give a copy of the most updated version of your Memorandum of Intent to your attorney, or another appropriate person, so it can be easily located when needed.

Your attorney will keep a copy in your file and, when the need arises, share that document with your child's caregiver and trustee(s). The document will be used to interpret your trust and to ensure your child gets the most personalized, responsible care possible.

INTENT

This Memorandum of Intent ("Memorandum") provides guidance to the guardian(s) of any child of ours with respect to decisions, choices, and our wishes regarding our child's care, as well as to the trustee of any trust we may leave for that child's benefit. It is intended to be binding to the greatest extent possible; however, we recognize that situations may change and unexpected circumstances may arise, so we request that all parties involved act in accordance with the intent we set forth in this memorandum. We appoint the guardian(s) of our minor child to carry out our wishes and desires as expressed within this Memorandum and direct our trustee of the _____, dated _____, to support our guardian(s) to the greatest extent possible in honoring our wishes set forth in this Memorandum.

Our estate plan includes a _____, a _____, and _____. Should this memorandum conflict with any provision of our primary estate planning documents, our _____ shall take precedence, followed by our _____, (etc.)

INTERESTED PARTIES

We are providing the following information to notify our family, friends, and affiliated organizations of our child's new guardianship.

Upon our child's being placed in a guardian's custody, please notify the following family members of our death or incapacity, and of the location of our child as soon as practicable:

	NAME	PHONE NUMBER	ADDRESS
1			
2			
3			
4			
5			

Upon our child's being placed in a guardian's custody, please notify the following friends and non-family members of our death or incapacity, and of the location of our child as soon as practicable:

	NAME	PHONE NUMBER	ADDRESS
1			
2			
3			
4			
5			

Upon our child's being placed in a guardian's custody, please notify the following organizations of our death or incapacity, and of the location of our child as soon as practicable:

	NAME	PHONE NUMBER	ADDRESS
1			
2			
3			
4			
5			

MISCELLANEOUS INSTRUCTIONS

_____

_____

_____

_____

_____

_____

_____

_____

_____

_____

IMPORTANT INFORMATION REGARDING OUR CHILD

Name: _____

Date of Birth: _____ Age: _____

Place of Birth: _____

Medical information

Primary Physician (location of medical records): _____

_____

_____

_____

Any medical conditions/required treatments:

_____

_____

_____

_____

_____

_____

_____

_____

_____

Child's therapist(s)

(1) Name of Therapist: _____

_____

_____

Type of Therapy: _____

_____

_____

Frequency of Therapy: _____

_____

_____

• • •

(2) Name of Therapist: _____

_____

_____

Type of Therapy: _____

_____

_____

Frequency of Therapy: _____

_____

_____

• • •

(3) Name of Therapist: _____

_____

_____

Type of Therapy: _____

_____

_____

Frequency of Therapy: _____

_____

_____

(4) Name of Therapist: _____

_____

_____

Type of Therapy: _____

_____

_____

Frequency of Therapy: _____

_____

_____

• • •

(5) Name of Therapist: _____

_____

_____

Type of Therapy: _____

_____

_____

Frequency of Therapy: _____

_____

_____

SCHOOL INFORMATION

Child's school and extracurricular programs:

_____

_____

_____

_____

_____

_____

_____

_____

RELIGION/SPIRITUALITY

Our child has been raised in the following religion, tradition, beliefs:

_____

_____

_____

_____

_____

_____

_____

It is important that my/our child (please check all that apply) . . .

☐ Continue to receive education in the religion above.

☐ Be free to learn and follow their own conscience with regard to religion and spirituality.

☐ Observe the following holidays:

- _____

- _____

- _____

- _____

- _____

- _____

- _____

- _____

☐ Participate in the following religious community:

- _____

- _____

- _____

- _____

- _____
- _____
- _____
- _____
- _____

EDUCATION

We strongly prefer that our child attend (please check all that apply) . . .

☐ The local public school.

☐ The following public school: _____
_____

☐ The following private school: _____
_____

☐ Other: _____
_____
_____

We urge child's guardian to monitor our child's education by (please check all that apply) . . .

☐ Attending all conferences.

☐ Attending most family activities.

☐ Volunteering at our child's school.

☐ Visiting our child's school frequently.

☐ Other: _____

_____

_____

We hope the guardian will help our child develop educationally by:

☐ Discussing all report cards carefully.

☐ Rewarding educational success.

☐ Helping our child to identify his/her interests and to pursue them inside and outside of the classroom.

☐ Rounding out our child's education by providing opportunities outside of the classroom to enjoy:

    ☐ nature

    ☐ athletics

    ☐ cultural events and places

    ☐ music

    ☐ national travel

    ☐ international travel

    ☐ other: _____

_____

DISCIPLINE

It is important to us that our child be disciplined in a manner consistent with our values.

[We believe that a child should not be punished for developmentally appropriate behaviors. Rather, we prefer that our guardian use distraction, redirection, negotiation, or another non-punitive method of modifying our child's behavior so that the guardian and our child can live together in peace.]

The following methods of discipline are totally unacceptable to us, and if our guardian feels he or she requires these methods, we wish that person to decline to accept guardianship of our children:

_____

_____

_____

_____

_____

_____

_____

_____

_____

_____

_____

_____

_____

The following methods of discipline are those we use most frequently because we believe they are appropriate and effective:

_____

_____

_____

_____

_____

_____

_____

_____

PARENTING RESOURCES

The following resources (books, organizations, media, etc.) have been helpful to us as we have developed our parenting philosophy. We encourage our child's guardian(s) to consider these resources for himself or herself:

_____

_____

_____

_____

_____

_____

_____

_____

MISCELLANEOUS INSTRUCTIONS

_____

_____

_____

_____

_____

_____

_____

_____

_____

Dated: _____ day of _____, 202__.

_____

Parent's Name

_____

Parent's Name

GUIDANCE TO TRUSTEE OF SPECIAL NEEDS TRUST, ALTERNATIVE VERSION

LETTER OF INTENT FOR:

_____

WRITTEN BY:

_____

[Relationship to the person with the disability—
mother, father or other family member]

DATE:

_____

TO WHOM IT MAY CONCERN:

INFORMATION ABOUT

(FATHER'S NAME)

GENERAL INFORMATION	
Full Name:	Social Security #:
Complete Address:	
Home Phone #:	Work Phone #:
Date of Birth:	Place of Birth:
City/Town/Country Raised:	Fluent Languages:
Religion:	Race:
Blood Type:	U.S. Citizen?

MARITAL STATUS	
Where Marriage Took Place:	Date:
# of Children from Marriage:	

PREVIOUS OR SUBSEQUENT MARRIAGES – INFO

Name of Other Spouse:	Date of Birth: Date of Marriage:
Children from Previous Marriage: (Name/Address/Phone #)	Dates of Birth:

FAMILY INFO

Provide complete names of father's siblings and parents.

For those still living, list addresses and phone numbers, as well as pertinent biographical information.

Name/Address/Phone #:	Biographical Info:

INFORMATION ABOUT

(MOTHER'S NAME)

GENERAL INFORMATION	
Full Name:	Social Security #:
Complete Address:	
Home Phone #:	Work Phone #:
Date of Birth:	Place of Birth:
City/Town/Country Raised:	Fluent Languages:
Religion:	Race:
Blood Type:	U.S. Citizen?

MARITAL STATUS	
Where Marriage Took Place:	Date:
# of Children from Marriage:	

PREVIOUS OR SUBSEQUENT MARRIAGES — INFO

Name of Other Spouse:	Date of Birth: Date of Marriage:
Name of Other Spouse:	Date of Birth: Date of Marriage:
Children from Previous Marriage (Name/Address/Phone #):	Dates of Birth:

FAMILY INFO

Provide complete names of mother's siblings and parents.
For those still living, list addresses and phone numbers, as well as pertinent biographical information.

Name/Address/Phone #:	Biographical Info:

INFORMATION ABOUT

_____

(CHILD'S NAME)

GENERAL INFORMATION		
Full Name:	Likes to Be Called:	Social Security #:
Complete Address:		
Home Phone #:	Work Phone #:	
Weight:	Height:	
Shoe Size:	Clothing Sizes:	
Gender:	Race:	Fluent Languages:
Religion:		U.S. Citizen?

BIRTH INFORMATION

Complications:	Date:
	Time:
	Birth Weight:
	Place of Birth:
	City/Town Raised:

SIBLINGS

Provide complete names, addresses, and phone numbers of all sisters and brothers. Indicate which ones are closest to the person with a disability—both geographically and emotionally.

Name/Address/Phone #:	Comments:

MARITAL STATUS

Spouse's Name:	Date of Birth:
	Date of Marriage:
Name/Address/Phone # of Children from This Marriage:	Date of Birth:

PREVIOUS OR SUBSEQUENT MARRIAGES — INFO

Name of Other Spouse:	Date of Birth: Date of Marriage:
Name of Other Spouse:	Date of Birth: Date of Marriage:
Children from Previous Marriage (Name/Address/Phone #)	Dates of Birth:

OTHER RELATIONSHIPS
List specific friends & relatives your child knows and likes, and describe relationship.

Name/Address/Phone #:	Relationship:

GUARDIANS
Indicate whether your child has been declared incompetent and whether any guardians have been appointed. List name, address, phone number of each guardian and indicate whether that person is a guardian of the person or guardian of the estate, plenary or limited.

Name/Address/Phone #:	Guardianship Details:

SUCCESSOR GUARDIANS
If chosen, list full names, addresses, and phone numbers.

Name/Address/Phone #:	Guardianship Details:

ADVOCATES
List people, in order, whom you foresee acting as advocates for your child after your death.

Name/Address/Phone #/Relationship:	Comments:

TRUSTEE
Indicate whether you have set up a trust for your child and list the full names, addresses, and phone numbers of all trustees.

Name/Address/Phone #:	Comments:

REPRESENTATIVE PAYEE
Indicate whether your son or daughter has or needs a representative payee to manage public entitlements, such as Supplemental Security Income or Social Security.

Name/Address/Phone #:	Comments:

POWER OF ATTORNEY

If anyone has power of attorney, list name/address/phone, and indicate whether this is a durable power of attorney.

Name/Address/Phone #:	Details:

FINAL ARRANGEMENTS

Describe any arrangements that have been made for your child's funeral and burial. List the full names, addresses, and phone numbers of companies or individuals. Also list all payments made and specify what is covered. If no arrangements have been made, indicate your preferences.

MEDICAL HISTORY FOR

(CHILD'S NAME)

[Insert additional pages if needed to complete the requested information.]

DIAGNOSES: (List main diagnosis for condition.)
SEIZURES: (Indicate seizure history; list anything that may act as a trigger for seizure.)
FUNCTIONING: (Indicate your child's intellectual functioning level—mild, moderate, severe, profound, etc.)
VISION: (Indicate status—normal, glasses, impaired, legally blind, etc.)
HEARING: (Indicate status—normal, hearing aid, impaired, deaf, etc.)
SPEECH: (Indicate status; if child is non-verbal, specify the techniques of communication.)

MOBILITY: (Indicate level of mobility—normal, impaired, wheelchair, etc.)

BLOOD: (List blood type and any special problems concerning blood.)

INSURANCE: (List type, amount, policy number for medical insurance covering son/daughter. What is included in coverage now? Indicate how this would change upon the death of either parent. Make sure you include Medicare and Medicaid, if relevant.)

CURRENT PHYSICIANS: (List full names, types of practice, addresses, phone numbers, the average number of times your child visits them each year, the total charges from each doctor during the last year, and the amounts not covered by a third party [insurance].)

PREVIOUS PHYSICIANS: (List their full names, addresses, phone numbers, the type of practice, and the most common reasons they saw your child. Describe any important findings or treatment. Explain why you no longer choose to consult them.)

DENTIST: (List the name, address, and phone number of your child's dentist, as well as the frequency of exams. Indicate what special treatments or recommendations the dentist has made. Also, list the best alternatives for dental care in case the dentist is no longer available.)

NURSING NEEDS: (Indicate your child's needs for nursing care; list the reasons, procedures, nursing skill required, etc. Is this care usually provided at home, at a clinic, or in a doctor's office?)

MENTAL HEALTH: (If your child has visited a psychiatrist, psychologist, or mental health counselor, list the name of each professional, the frequency of visits, and the goals of the sessions. What types of therapy have been successful? What types have not worked?)

THERAPY: (Physical, Speech, Occupational? List purposes of each type, plus name, address, and phone number of each therapist. What assistive devices have been helpful? Has an occupational therapist evaluated your home to assist you in making it more accessible for your child?)

DIAGNOSTIC TESTING: (Info about all diagnostic testing done in the past—name, address, and phone number, test, testing dates, summary of findings. How often do you recommend that diagnostic testing be done? Where?)

GENETIC TESTING: (List the findings of all genetic tests of your child and relatives. Also list the name, address, phone number, and testing dates.)

IMMUNIZATIONS: (List the type and dates of all immunizations.)

DISEASES: (List all childhood diseases and the date of their occurrence. List any other infectious diseases your child has had in the past. List any infectious diseases your child currently has. Has your child been diagnosed as a carrier for any disease?)

ALLERGIES: (List all allergies and current treatments. Describe past treatments and their effectiveness.)

OTHER PROBLEMS: (Describe any special problems your child has, such as bad reactions to the sun or staph infections if he or she becomes too warm.)

PROCEDURES: (Describe any helpful hygiene procedures such as cleaning wax out of ears periodically, trimming toenails, or cleaning teeth. Are these procedures currently done at home or by a doctor or other professional? What do you recommend for the future?)

OPERATIONS: (List all operations and the dates and places of their occurrence.)

HOSPITALIZATION: (List any other periods of hospitalization your child has had. List the people you recommend to monitor your child's voluntary or involuntary hospitalizations and to act as liaison with doctors.)

BIRTH CONTROL: (If your son or daughter uses any kind of birth control pill or device, list the type, dates used, and doctor prescribing it.)

DEVICES: (Does your son or daughter need any adaptive or prosthetic devices, such as glasses, braces, shoes, hearing aids, or artificial limbs?)

MEDICATIONS: (List all prescription medications currently being taken, plus the dosage and purpose of each one. Describe your feelings about the medications. List any particular medications that have proved effective for particular problems that have occurred frequently in the past and the doctor prescribing the medicine. List medications that have not worked well in the past and the reasons. Include a list of medications that have caused allergic reactions.)

OTC: (List any over-the-counter medications that have proved helpful, such as vitamins or dandruff shampoo. Describe the conditions helped by these medications and frequency of use.)

MONITORING: (Indicate whether your child needs someone to monitor the taking of medications or to apply ointments, etc. If so, who currently does this? What special qualifications would this person need?)

PROCUREMENT: (Does your child need someone to procure medications?)

DIET: (If your child has a special diet of any kind, please describe it in detail and indicate the reasons for the diet. If there is no special diet, you might want to include tips about what works well for avoiding weight gain and for following the general guidelines of a balanced, healthy diet. You might also describe the foods your child likes best and where the recipes for these foods can be found.)

ADDITIONAL COMMENTS:

WHAT WORKS WELL FOR

(CHILD'S NAME)

[Insert additional pages if needed to complete the requested information.]

HOUSING

PRESENT:
Describe current living situation and indicate advantages/disadvantages.

PAST:
Describe past living situations. What worked? What didn't?

FUTURE:
Describe in detail any plans that have been made for future living situations. Describe your idea of the best living arrangement for your child at various ages or stages. Prioritize your desires. For each age or state, which of the following living arrangements would you prefer?

DESCRIPTION:	PRIORITIZE:	
		A relative's home (which relative?)
		Supported living in an apartment or house with hours of supervision.
		A group home with no more than ____ residents.

		A state institution (which one?)
		A private institution (which one?)
		Adult foster care.
		Parent-owned housing with ____ hours of supervision.
		Housing owned by your child with ____ hours of supervision, etc.

SIZE:

Indicate the minimum and maximum sizes of any residential options that you consider suitable.

ADAPTATION:

Does the residence need to be adapted with ramps, grab bars, or other assistive devices?

COMMUNITY:

List the types of places that would need to be conveniently reached from your child's home. Include favorite restaurants, shopping areas, recreation areas, libraries, museums, banks, etc.

DAILY LIVING SKILLS

IPP:
Describe your child's current Individual Program Plan.

CURRENT ACTIVITIES:
Describe an average daily schedule. Also, describe activities usually done on "days off."

AVERAGE MORNING:	AVERAGE AFTERNOON:
"DAY OFF" MORNING:	"DAY OFF" AFTERNOON:

MONITORING:
Discuss thoroughly whether someone needs to monitor or help with the following items.

ITEMS:	DESCRIBE HELP NEEDED:
Self-care skills like personal hygiene or dressing.	
Domestic activities like housekeeping, cooking, shopping for clothes, doing laundry, or shopping for groceries and cleaning supplies.	
Transportation for daily commuting, recreational activities, and emergencies.	
Reinforcement of social and interpersonal activities with others to develop social skills.	
Other areas.	

CAREGIVERS' ATTITUDES:
Describe how you would like caregivers to treat matters like sanitation, social skills (including table manners, appearance, and relationships with the opposite sex). What values do you want caregivers to demonstrate?

SELF-ESTEEM:
Describe how you best reinforce self-esteem, discussing how you praise and set realistic goals.

SLEEP HABITS:
How much sleep does your son/daughter require? Does he/she have any special sleep habits or methods of waking up?

PERSONAL FINANCES:
Indicate whether your son/daughter needs assistance with personal banking, bill payments, and budgeting. If so, how much help is needed?

ALLOWANCE:
Indicate whether you recommend a personal allowance for your son/daughter. If so, how much? Also, list your recommendations about supervision of how the allowance is spent.

EDUCATION

SCHOOLS:
List the schools your child has attended at various ages and the level of education completed in each program. Include early intervention, day care, and transition programs.

SCHOOL	AGE ATTENDED/LEVEL COMPLETED

CURRENT PROGRAMS:
List the specific programs, schools, and teachers your son/daughter has now. Include address and phone numbers.

SCHOOL:	ADDRESS/PHONE:
TEACHER:	

SPECIFIC PROGRAMS:

ACADEMICS:
Estimate the grade level of your son/daughter's academic skills in reading, writing, math, etc. List any special abilities.

READING:	WRITING:

MATH:

SPECIAL ABILITIES:

EMPHASIS:
Describe the types of educational emphasis (such as academic, vocational, or community-based) on which your son or daughter currently concentrates. What educational emphasis do you think would be best for the future?

INTEGRATION:
Describe the extent that your child has been in regular classes or schools during his/her education. What are your desires for the future? What kinds of undesirable conditions would alter those desires?

DAY PROGRAM OR WORK

PRESENT:
Describe current day program and/or job.

PAST:
Describe past experiences. What worked? What didn't? Why?

FUTURE:
Discuss future objectives. Prioritize your desires.

ASSISTANCE:
Indicate to what extent, if any, your son/daughter needs assistance in searching for a job, in being trained, in becoming motivated, and in receiving support or supervision on the job.

LEISURE & RECREATION

STRUCTURED RECREATION:
Describe your son/daughter's structured recreational activities. List favorite activities and favorite people involved in each activity.

FAVORITE ACTIVITY:	FAVORITE PEOPLE INVOLVED:

UNSTRUCTURED ACTIVITIES:
What are your child's favorite means of self-expression, interest, and skills (going to movies, listening to music, dancing, collecting baseball cards, painting, bowling, riding a bicycle, roller skating, etc.)? List the favorite people involved in each activity.

ACTIVITY:	FAVORITE PEOPLE INVOLVED:

VACATIONS:
Describe your son/daughter's favorite vacations. Who organizes them? How often do they occur, and when are they usually scheduled?

FITNESS:
If your son/daughter participates in a fitness program, please describe the type of program, as well as the details about where and when it takes place and who oversees it.

RELIGION

FAITH:
List the religion of your son/daughter, if any. Indicate any membership in a particular church or synagogue.

FAITH:	CHURCH/SYNAGOGUE MEMBERSHIP:

CLERGY:

List any ministers, priests, or rabbis familiar with your son/daughter. Include the names of the churches or synagogues involved and their addresses and phone numbers. Also indicate how often your child might like to be visited by these people.

MINISTERS/PRIESTS/RABBIS:	CHURCH/SYNAGOGUE ADDRESS & PHONE:

OF TIMES TO VISIT:

PARTICIPATION:

Estimate how frequently your son/daughter would like to participate in services and other activities of the church or synagogue. Indicate how this might change over time. Also describe any major, valued events in the past.

RIGHTS & VALUES

Please list the rights and values that should be accorded your son/daughter. Some examples are:

- To be free from harm, physical restraint, isolation, abuse, and excessive medication.
- To refuse behavior modification techniques that cause pain.
- To have age-appropriate clothing and appearance.
- To have staff, if any, demonstrate respect and caring, and to refrain from using demeaning language.

OTHER CONCERNS

SERVICES AND BENEFITS:

List any services or benefits that your child receives. These might be services for children with physical impairments, developmental disability services, clinics sponsored by support groups, early periodic screening, diagnosis and treatment, employment assistance, food stamps, housing assistance, legal assistance, library services, maternal and child health services, Medicaid, Medicare, Project Head Start, special education, Title XX service programs, transportation assistance, or vocational rehabilitation services.

GAPS:

Indicate whether any services or benefits are needed but are not being received by your son/ daughter. Indicate whether plans exist to improve the current delivery of services or to obtain needed benefits.

EXPENSES:

List all expenses and indicate who is paying for expenses (child, parents, guardians, trustees, third parties such as insurance companies, etc.).

EXPENSE:	AMOUNT:	PAID BY:
HOUSING		
EDUCATION		
HEALTH CARE		
RECREATION		
VOCATION TRAINING		
PERSONAL SPENDING		

CHANGES:
Indicate how your child's financial picture would change if one or both parents died. Be sure to list any additional cash benefits to which your child definitely would be entitled. Also, list any cash benefits for which your child might be eligible.

ADDITIONAL MEDICAL INFORMATION:

INSERT A PICTURE OF YOUR CHILD HERE:

ADDITIONAL COMMENTS:

GUIDANCE FOR TRUSTEE OF FAMILY PROTECTION TRUST

STATEMENT OF INTENT

[Provide details as needed.]

Statements of Intent with regard to the administration of the family protection trusts for our children:

1. We do/do not want the income earned on the trust to be distributed to my children.

2. We do/do not want the trustee to use trust funds to pay for vacations and leisure activities of the beneficiaries.

3. We do/do not want the trustee to use trust funds for my children's and grandchildren's education.

4. We do/do not want the trustee to use trust funds for my children's and grandchildren's living expenses, including rent, mortgage, utilities, food, and clothing.

5. We do/do not want the trustee to use trust funds for my children's and grandchildren's home maintenance.

6. We do/do not want the trustee to provide my children and grandchildren with luxury items, such as boats, vehicles, or jewelry.

7. We do/do not want the trustee to preserve the assets in the trust for the benefit of the remainderman (grandchildren and great grandchildren).

8. We do/do not want the trustee to use the trust assets for medical expenses of my children and grandchildren, including the monthly cost of insurance.

9. We do/do not want the trustee to pay for insurance if it benefits my children and grandchildren and their spouses and children.

_____

Grantor

_____

Grantor

INSTRUCTIONS REGARDING HOUSE IN TRUST

LETTER OF INSTRUCTIONS

By this letter deposited with the trustees of The _____ Trust under an Agreement of Trust established _____, as amended (the "Trust"), I, _____, of _____, _____ (the "Settlor"), married to _____, express my instructions and wishes with respect to the disposition of the trust property upon the death of the survivor of my spouse and myself, but without imposing any legal obligations.

If the trust property shall include real estate in _____, _____, to the extent practicable, such real estate shall be maintained for the use and enjoyment of my child, _____ ("[child's first name]"). If the trust property does not include real estate in _____, _____, I hope that my trustees will purchase a similar parcel of real estate during [child's first name]'s lifetime, so that he or she may live comfortably and without stress, in a similar situation as he or she does now.

It is my hope and intention that the trustees rent that part of the _____ real estate, or similarly purchased real estate, not used by [child's first name], and add any rental proceeds that may be paid on such real estate to the Trust. In addition, _____ may direct the trustees to sell the _____ real estate and purchase similar real estate for [child's first name] to reside as described above. If the trustees, hopefully in consultation with [child's first name], agree to sell the property, the sales proceeds in excess of the purchase cost of the similar real estate should be added to the other trust property held by the trustees.

As to non–real-estate trust property, the trustees shall first pay trust expenses and real estate taxes from this real estate described above. Other than life necessities, health, education, maintenance, and support, it is my hope and intention that the trustees consider the other available resources of any beneficiary, and a "spendthrift" standard should be applied to all distributions. Furthermore, it is my wish that the trust principal should only be drawn from as a last resort.

Lastly, to the extent possible, it is my hope and intention that the independent trustee shall consult with all relevant family members and attorneys before making distributions to [child's first name] or any beneficiary, that may affect his or her care or any future or continuing qualification for governmental benefits to which he or she may be entitled.

EXECUTED, in duplicate, under seal on _____, 202__.

_____

Settlor and Trustee

INDEX

Made in United States
North Haven, CT
22 July 2024

55324618R00143